Medieval Britain

Conquest, power and people

Tony McAleavy

Adviser for Humanities, Gloucestershire

The right of the University of Cambridge to print and sell all manner of books was granted by Henry VIII in 1534. The University has printed and published continuously since 1584.

CAMBRIDGE UNIVERSITY PRESS

Cambridge   New York   Port Chester   Melbourne   Sydney

For Daniel and Patrick

Published by the Press Syndicate of the University of Cambridge
The Pitt Building, Trumpington Street, Cambridge CB2 1RP
40 West 20th Street, New York, NY 10011-4211, USA
10 Stamford Road, Oakleigh, Melbourne 3166, Australia

© Cambridge University Press 1991

First published 1991

Printed and bound in Great Britain by Scotprint, Musselburgh

British Library cataloguing in publication data
McAleavy, Tony
Medieval Britain: conquest, power and people
(Cambridge history programme).
1. Great Britain. History, 1066–1485
I. Title
941.02

ISBN 0 521 40708 7

Text illustrations by Alison Wisenfeld and Sue Shields
Maps by Chris Etheridge

Picture research by Callie Kendall

Notice to teachers
Many of the sources used in this textbook have
been adapted or abridged from the original.

Acknowledgements

Thanks are due to the following for permission to reproduce photographs:

p 5 The President and Fellows of Corpus Christi College, Oxford/photo: The Bodleian Library, Oxford. pp 8, 18, 20, 26, 30, 35, 40, 45, 55, 56, 63, 72, 75 By permission of the British Library. pp 10, 11, 13 Tapisserie de Bayeux et avec autorisation speciale de la Ville de Bayeux. p 15 Reproduced from the facsimile edition of the Domesday Book, published by Alecto Editions Ltd. pp 16, 22 The Master and Fellows of Corpus Christi College, Cambridge. p 27 (L) Private Collection. p 27 (R) Mansell Collection. p 29 The Pierpont Morgan Library, New York, M. 638, f. 10r; © The Pierpont Morgan Library 1991. p 31 The Master and Fellows of Trinity College, Cambridge. p 33 National Portrait Gallery, London. p 34 Delaroche: Enfants d'Edouard I; Louvre; © Photo R. M. N. p 39 Cambridge University Collection of Air Photographs. p 39 The Dean and Chapter of Durham. p 40 MS Add A.46, f.4v, The Bodleian Library, Oxford. p 43 Bibliotheque Nationale, Paris. p 45 MS Douce 195, f. 111r, The Bodleian Library, Oxford. p 43 Bibliotheque Nationale, Paris. p 45 MS Douce 195, f. 111r, The Bodleian Library, Oxford. p 49 Courtesy of the Trustees of the British Museum. p 53 Society of Antiquaries, London. p 54 MS Ee.3.59, f.4r; by permission of the Syndics of the Cambridge University Library. pp 58, 71, 76 A. F. Kersting. p 62 English Heritage. p 64 Edinburgh University Library. p 65 © Centre de l'Image, Assistance Publique - Hopitaux de Paris. p 66 Giraudon; Tres Riches Herues de duc de Berry by Jean Colombe; Musee Conde, Chantilly. p 67 Bibliotheque Royale de Belgique, Brussels. p 70 MS 177, f.60r, Trinity Colleg, Dublin. p 74 Reproduction by permission of The Huntington Library, San Marino, California.

Cover illustration: 'The Battle of Agincourt'. MS 6, f.243, reproduced by permission of the Archbishop of Canterbury and the Trustees of Lambeth Palace Library.

Every effort has been made to reach copyright holders. The publishers would be pleased to hear from anyone whose rights they have unwittingly infringed.

Contents

The dream of Henry I

Henry I, a king of England in the twelfth century, once had a nightmare that frightened him very much. He told his doctor all about the dream, his doctor told a friend, and the friend drew some pictures to illustrate the dream. These pictures give us an unusual glimpse into the mind of a medieval king.

What problems faced rulers in the Middle Ages?

A king and his people

Henry dreamed that while he was asleep three groups of people came and attacked him. The different groups were: the leaders of the Church, the rich nobles and the common people. It is no coincidence that Henry was frightened of being attacked by these three types of people. Conflict between the king and different sections of society was common throughout the Middle Ages.

In this book you will find examples of each stage of Henry's nightmare becoming a reality. You will also be able to find out about the daily life of men and women in the years 1066–1500; and how some people did well while others suffered, depending on which group they happened to be in.

Who were the nobles?

Most money and power belonged to a few hundred land-owning families. Together they were known as the nobility. The very richest nobles were also called barons. They were warlike, and had their own soldiers. When they were not fighting for the king, they sometimes fought against him. Successful kings got on well with their nobles. Those who were disliked by the nobles, such as King John in the thirteenth century, had a difficult and unhappy time.

The power of the Church

Religion was far more important to medieval men and women than it is today. Each village was dominated by its church, and the village priest had a great impact on the way in which people lived. The Church was very rich and powerful and owned vast amounts of land. Sometimes the leaders of the Church (the Pope, the archbishops and the bishops) argued with the king. For example, Archbishop Thomas Becket was murdered by the king's men in 1170 after a big argument with Henry II.

A mixture of 'common people'

Anyone who was not royal or noble or in the Church was part of the 'common people'. This included rich merchants in towns, as well as poor farming families in the countryside. Wealthy townsfolk grew more powerful during the Middle Ages, although they were nowhere near as strong as the nobles. Poor country folk had no say in the way in which the country was run. Occasionally, they turned to violence to make their voices heard. This happened in the great Peasants' Revolt of 1381.

SOURCE A

Henry I's dream: three groups of people would rise up and destroy him. These pictures were drawn by the monk, John of Worcester, the friend of Henry's doctor. They are taken from the *Chronicle of John of Worcester*, twelfth century.

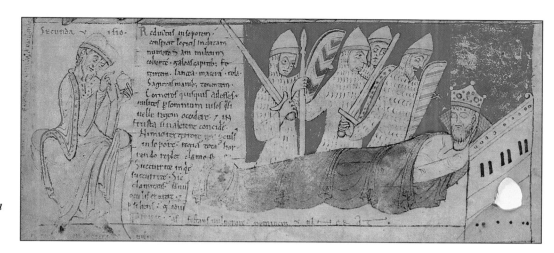

Henry is attacked by the nobles. This was a constant worry for medieval kings.

Like many rulers, Henry often argued with the Church. Here he dreams of attack by the clergy. The bishops and abbots are pointing their staves at him.

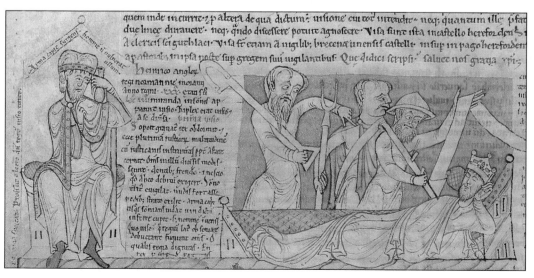

The common people had little power, but occasionally they rose up in rebellion. What weapons are the people carrying in Henry's dream?

A chronicle of the

An invading army of Normans conquered England in the eleventh century. They were tough soldiers and the ordinary English were badly treated. Castles were built by the Normans in many places to stop the English fighting back. The Normans soon began to move into Wales, Scotland and Ireland.

1066 William the Conqueror and his Norman army win at the Battle of Hastings

Kings were powerful people in the Middle Ages. They expected to be obeyed. This sometimes led to arguments with Church leaders, who did not like being ordered about by kings. Henry II argued with Archbishop Thomas Becket. Some of Henry's men went to Canterbury Cathedral and murdered Becket.

1170 Thomas Becket, Archbishop of Canterbury, is murdered

The richest nobles were called barons and they were very powerful. King John annoyed his barons by taking lots of money from them. They rebelled and fought against him. They made him sign a document called Magna Carta. It said that, in future, a king was not allowed to do exactly as he pleased.

1215 King John signs the Magna Carta

From the early Middle Ages, kings had regular meetings with their barons. In thirteenth-century England their meetings grew larger and were attended by men from all counties and large towns. This was the beginning of Parliament. They discussed many things, especially how much tax the king should get.

Thirteenth–century English kings hold the first meetings of Parliament

struggle for power

The kings of England tried to take over Ireland, Scotland and Wales. Henry II conquered Ireland, but the English soon lost real control. Wales was successfully taken over by Edward I, but the Scots beat his son at Bannockburn and Scotland stayed free.

1314 The Scottish army defeat the English at Bannockburn

Ordinary men and women had little power in the Middle Ages. This changed for a few days in 1381 when a great rebellion happened in the English countryside. The rebels captured London and killed government ministers. The Revolt ended when their leader, Wat Tyler, was stabbed to death.

1381 The Peasants' Revolt sweeps southern England

The so-called 'Hundred Years War' was fought between England and France. English kings said that they should also be rulers of France. At times the English did well, but in the end they were defeated. Failure and the high cost of war made many people in England very unhappy with the government.

1337–1453 England and France are at war

There was a long and violent argument between 1459 and 1485 over who should be king of England. At times different sides fought each other and these battles became known as the 'Wars of the Roses'. Peace returned in 1485, when Henry VII took over from Richard III. The new king belonged to the Tudor family.

1485 The death of Richard III ends the 'Wars of the Roses'

7

Britain before the Norman Conquest

> *After the Romans left Britain in the early fifth century, the island was invaded by people known as the Anglo-Saxons. Over many years, they came to control most of the area we call England.*

SOURCE A

Anglo-Saxon kings were very powerful. Here one king meets with his nobles to judge a criminal. What did they decide to do to him?

A land of Anglo-Saxon and Celtic people

The Anglo-Saxon invaders came from the area of northern Germany and Denmark. They were not Christian but worshipped a large number of gods. In the seventh century the Anglo-Saxons became Christian.

Ireland, Wales and much of Scotland were untouched by the early waves of Anglo-Saxon settlers. The Celtic peoples of these lands had been Christian for a long time. They spoke Celtic languages, which were very different from the language of the Anglo-Saxons. In its early days, Anglo-Saxon England was divided up into a number of small kingdoms. Some modern counties get their names from these kingdoms: Sussex was the land of the 'South Saxons'.

The impact of the Vikings

In the ninth century, Vikings from Denmark and Norway swept across Britain and Ireland. Many of them came to stay. The Vikings destroyed nearly all of the Anglo-Saxon kingdoms. Only one kingdom survived – the land of Wessex in the south-west of England. Eventually the kings of Wessex became the kings of all England.

The end of an era

The Anglo-Saxon world came to an end in 1066 after the death of the king, Edward the Confessor. He had no son, and it was not clear who should succeed him to the throne. His kingdom was a rich prize. It was wealthy and peaceful. It had a strong government that was able to get lots of money from people in taxes. It is hardly surprising that many men wanted to be the next king.

1066: the Conquest

> On 5 January 1066 Edward the Confessor, the king of England, died without children. Three different men said that they should be the next king. By the end of the year, two of the men had been killed in violent battles and the third, William of Normandy, became king.
>
> Why was William the winner of this struggle to the death?

Contender No 1: William, the Duke of Normandy

Contender No 2: Harold Godwineson, the richest nobleman in England

Contender No 3: Harald Hardraada, the king of Norway

Harold – the early favourite

At first Harold Godwineson, the richest nobleman in England, looked like the most likely winner. He was the only one of the three in England when Edward died. Look at the following source and work out what other advantages he had.

SOURCE A

'Before the death of Edward, Harold Godwineson was known as the under-king and Edward had named him as the man who should be the next king. After Edward's burial, Harold was chosen as king by the most important nobles of all England. When he became king, Harold immediately got rid of bad laws and made new, good laws. He showed himself to be religious and kind to good people, but very tough on those who broke the law.'

Florence of Worcester, a twelfth-century English monk

SOURCE B

This description of Harold was written by a Norman who supported William as king.

'Harold was stained with wickedness. He was a cruel murderer, who was only interested in money and was proud of the loot he had stolen. He was an enemy of good laws and good acts.'

William of Poitiers, *The Deeds of William*, about 1070

Harald Hardraada and William invade

While Harold Godwineson passed new laws to show that he was in charge, his enemies got ready to invade England. By late summer in 1066, both Harald Hardraada and William of Normandy had ships and men waiting for the right wind to take them across to England. The first invader to arrive was Harald Hardraada, the king of Norway. Hardraada joined forces with some English people who did not like Harold Godwineson.

SOURCE D

'Harald Hardraada arrived suddenly on the River Tyne with more than five hundred big ships. When King Harold Godwineson heard this, he marched north with great speed. As he came towards York with thousands of good soldiers, he met the Norwegians in battle at Stamford Bridge. He killed Harald and most of his army. At this moment, King Harold was told that William had arrived with a huge army of men from all over France.'

Florence of Worcester, early twelfth century

The wind changes

William was lucky. His invasion fleet crossed the Channel at just the time when Harold Godwineson was hundreds of miles away in Yorkshire. William was only able to do this because the direction of the wind changed while Harold was in the north.

Bloodshed at Hastings

Exactly two weeks after the Norman army crossed the Channel, William and Harold met at the Battle of Hastings. What can we learn from the following sources about why William won the Battle of Hastings?

SOURCE E

The author of this extract was a Norman monk.

'William filled his ships with mighty horses and very brave men. He landed at Pevensey, where he immediately built a castle. He hurried to Hastings, where he built another castle.'

William of Jumieges, *Deeds of the Dukes of Normandy*, written in about 1070

SOURCE F

'When Harold heard of William's landing, he marched with great haste from York to London. Before even half of his army had arrived, he marched on to Sussex with all speed. A battle began near Hastings before Harold had time to get most of his soldiers in position.'

Florence of Worcester, early twelfth century

◄ *William the Conqueror. Can you find evidence for each of these explanations of why he ended up the winner?*

10

SOURCE G

The Bayeux Tapestry says in Latin 'Harold the King was killed'. Which one do you think is Harold?

SOURCE H

'Duke William and his men came slowly up the hill, raining death upon the English with their arrows. The English fought back bravely, throwing spears, axes and stones. The Normans were about to retreat when Duke William pushed himself to the front and said, "Look at me. I am still alive and, with God's help, I shall be the winner." With these words he made the Normans brave again.'

William of Poitiers, *The Deeds of William,* about 1070

SOURCE I

'All the English were on foot. The Normans had foot-soldiers, archers and cavalry with horses. The battle seemed to go one way and then the other while Harold lived. But then Harold was killed by an arrow which pierced his brain. When the English knew Harold was dead, they began to run away.'

The Anglo-Saxon Chronicle, eleventh century

● Can you see examples of good decisions by William and bad decisions by Harold?

1 Arrange these events into the order in which they happened:

♦ William's invasion of England
♦ the Battle of Hastings
♦ the death of Edward the Confessor
♦ Harald Hardraada's invasion of England.

2 Look at Sources A and B. What different things do they say about Harold Godwineson? How can you explain this?

3 Which source is most useful for finding out what happened at the Battle of Hastings, Source G, Source H or Source I? Explain.

4 Historians think that there were a number of reasons why William won the fight for control of England. Using information from this unit, show how the following factors helped William to victory:

♦ William was lucky
♦ Harold Godwineson made mistakes
♦ William was brave.

Find two more reasons of your own.

Write a few more lines to explain which reasons you think were the most important.

The Normans in power

You are William the Conqueror. It is 1066 and you have just won the Battle of Hastings. You now have three main aims:

a to crush the English rebels so that they cannot get rid of you as king

b to find out exactly what England is like so that you can get as much money as possible in rent and taxes from your new land

c to reward the Normans who fought with you and helped you to win the Battle of Hastings. What would you do to achieve these aims? Would you be harsh or generous to your enemies? Compare your ideas with those of other people in your class.

Now study the following section to find out what William actually did.

Dealing with the English rebels

Although the Normans won the Battle of Hastings in 1066, it was a long time before they had control over all England. Many English people did not want a foreign king.

SOURCE A

'The English who survived looked for chances to ambush the hated Normans. They attacked and killed them in secret in woods and other lonely places.'

Richard fitz Nigel, a twelfth-century writer

Castles far and wide

We have already seen that one of the first things William did when he reached England was to build castles at Pevensey and Hastings. After the Battle of Hastings, the Normans put up new castles all over England. With a castle as a base, Norman soldiers could patrol the local countryside and keep the English people under control. Norman soldiers forced English people to build the castles for them. Hundreds of people had their houses pulled down to make space for the new castles.

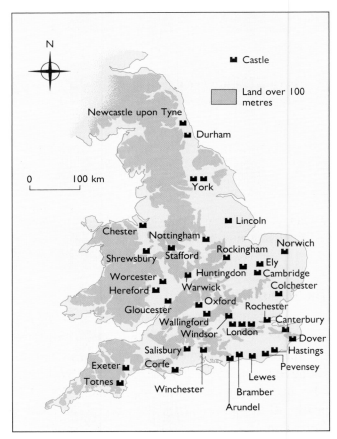

Castles built by William and the Norman soldiers.

● What do you think the English felt about the new castles?

The 'harrying of the North'

Opposition to the Norman take-over was strongest in the north of England. In 1069 there was a rebellion against William that began in Yorkshire. William replied by marching from Nottingham to York, and it was said that he killed every man he met. After capturing York, the Normans spread out across the North, burning down every village and destroying all crops and food. Many people starved to death as a result. This was called the 'harrying of the North'. After this there were no more large-scale rebellions against the Normans.

SOURCE B

This is William's own description of the 'harrying of the North' according to an early twelfth-century writer.

'I was hard on the English. I attacked the northern counties like a hungry lion. I burned the houses, crops and goods of anyone there, and butchered all their animals. This led to a cruel famine, in which many thousands died.'

The words of William the Conqueror on his death-bed, according to Orderic Vitalis, an Anglo-Norman monk, early twelfth–century

● Can you think of a reason why he would speak like this as he lay dying?

The Normans seize the land

After the Battle of Hastings, William believed that the whole of England was his property. He took the farms from most of the old English nobles. He gave much of the land to men from Normandy who had fought with him at Hastings. By 1086 nearly all the farmland and villages in the country were under Norman control. At the same time William gave all the important jobs in the government and the Church to Normans. Once the English had lost their land and their jobs, it was very difficult for them to fight against the Normans.

SOURCE C

The Normans burn down an English house and force a woman and child to flee. Why was this a common sight in northern England in 1069?

The making of the Domesday Book

In 1085, William ordered a huge survey of the land that he had conquered. When it was written up, it became known as the Domesday Book.

SOURCE D

'The king sent his men over all England into every county to find out how much land there was and how much tax should be paid from each county. This was done so carefully that there was not a single ox, cow or pig that was left out.'

The Anglo-Saxon Chronicle, eleventh century

The Domesday Book gave the Normans a great deal of information about the land that they had conquered.

● 'Domesday' means 'Day of Judgement'. Why do you think the Domesday Book was called this?

Opinions about William

William the Conqueror died in 1087. What did people think of him once he was dead? Look at the following sources to work out an answer.

SOURCE E

A monk in Normandy wrote this description of William shortly after his death.

'This king was one of the cleverest and greatest of all. No task ever put him off, no matter how difficult or dangerous it was.'

Anonymous monk of Caen, about 1090

SOURCE F

The Anglo-Saxon Chronicle was written by English monks who were sad that their country had been conquered.

'He had castles built, which was hard on poor men. The king was very strict, and he took much gold and silver from his people. He loved greediness above all.'

The Anglo-Saxon Chronicle, eleventh century

● Are you surprised that the Norman monk and the English monks say different things about William?

SOURCE G

Orderic Vitalis was born in England, but spent his working life as a monk in Normandy. One of his parents was English, the other Norman.

'William did much that should be praised. However, I cannot praise him for the "harrying of the North", during which both the guilty and the innocent died through starvation. This was cruel murder and he should have been punished for it.'

Orderic Vitalis, early twelfth century

SOURCE H

A modern historian has used some unusual evidence to argue that many people in England may have liked William.

'"William" became and remained the single most commonly recorded name in the twelfth century, which suggests that William the Conqueror was not as unpopular as the Anglo-Saxon Chronicle made out.'

M T Clanchy, *England and its Rulers*, 1983

SOURCE I

This is an extract from the most important study of William's life written in modern times.

'His brutalities and greed speak for themselves. But it would be quite wrong to see him as a crude ruffian. He was religious. He could be generous.'

D C Douglas, *William the Conqueror*, 1964

● What do modern historians think about William?

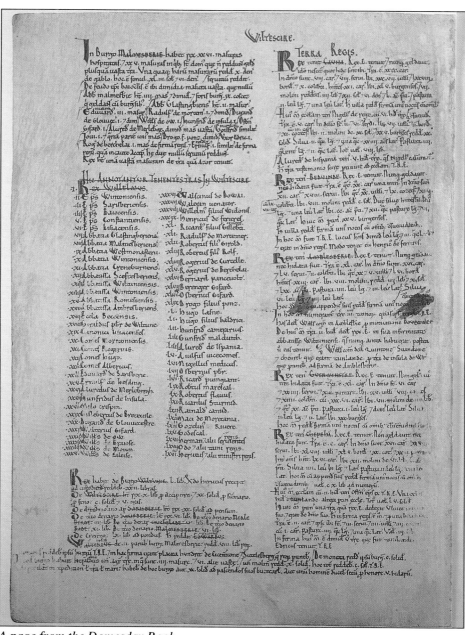

A page from the Domesday Book.

1 Using the information on pages 12 and 13 and Sources A–D, write down some facts about what William did.

2 Sources E–I give us opinions about William. Decide which sources are for William and which are against him. Which do you think are neither for nor against him?

3 Why do you think people in the Middle Ages and modern historians have different opinions of William and what he did?

4 What is *your* opinion of William and what he did?

Kings and Parliaments

This book covers nearly 500 years of history. During this long period of time some aspects of life changed a lot; other things changed little.

How far did the work of a king change during the Middle Ages?

Medieval kingship

Some aspects of a king's job changed very little between 1066 and 1500.

Landowner
The king owned huge amounts of land. Some land was farmed, and some was royal forest, used for hunting.

God's representative
People believed kings were chosen by God to rule over them. The king's power came directly from God.

Provider of justice
Kings were in charge of law and order and were supposed to punish criminals. As God's representative, kings were the highest source of justice in the land.

Spender
The king spent a lot of money. He paid for his castles, army, servants, retinue, clothing and jewellery. His money came from rents, feudal dues, fines, loans and taxes.

Warrior
People expected kings to lead a royal army in war.

Hunter
Most kings relaxed by spending many hours hunting.

Nomad
Medieval kings were always on the move from place to place. They stayed in castles, great monasteries, and sometimes camped in luxury tents. They were accompanied by a large retinue of servants.

Source A

The coronation of a medieval king. The coronation was a very important and holy ceremony. The king is sitting on his throne, dressed in fine robes. His bishops and nobles surround him. The Archbishop of Canterbury is standing to his left, touching his crown. We can just see some faces in the background. They represent the common people, watching their king from afar, behind iron bars. From a thirteenth-century manuscript.

What is the king holding? What do you think they might represent?

Kingship and change

In some ways the work and position of a king changed a great deal in the Middle Ages.

The work of central government became more complicated. Many new judges and civil servants were appointed by the king.

Kings needed more and more money to fight wars. By the late Middle Ages, kings needed permission from Parliament to get taxes from the people to pay for armies.

The rise of Parliament

One of the most important changes in government was the growth of Parliament. Kings like William the Conqueror used to meet regularly with the great nobles or barons for advice; this was called the Great Council. In the thirteenth century the Great Council became known as the Parliament (from the French word *parler* = talk). The barons said that if a king wanted more money in taxes then Parliament must give its permission.

Lords and Commons

At first the only members of Parliament were very rich nobles. This changed in the late thirteenth century when rich townsmen and local knights were invited. These people came to form the 'House of Commons'. Parliament grew in power when the country was at war because the king needed more money and had to get taxes from Parliament.

The model Parliament. Edward I called a Parliament in 1295. It became known as the 'model' Parliament because it had so many of the features of later Parliaments.

THE LORDS

The great barons
The richest nobles in the country.

Bishops and abbots
Leading members of the Church.

THE KING

Unlike today, Parliament only met when the king wanted it to.

The king ran the government. Parliament could not tell him what to do. However, they did have some power. They could stop taxes if they did not like what the king was doing.

THE COMMONS

The burgesses
The richest men of the towns, called burgesses, chose representatives to speak for them.

The knights
In each county the local knights elected representatives.

1 In what ways was the job of a king different from that of a modern monarch?

2 In what ways did the king's job hardly change during the Middle Ages?

3 In what ways did the king's job actually change during the Middle Ages?

4 Do you think the king became more or less powerful during the Middle Ages?

Murder in the cathedral

On 29 December 1170, Thomas Becket, the Archbishop of Canterbury, was murdered in Canterbury Cathedral by a group of knights loyal to King Henry II. Becket's violent death shocked people all over Europe.

Why was Becket murdered?

SOURCE A

Knights loyal to King Henry kill Becket. The priest on the right is Edward Grim, the writer of Source B. The picture was painted in about 1200, many years after the murder. Why did Becket become King Henry's deadly enemy?

An eye-witness account

We know a lot about the murder because there were several eye-witnesses who later wrote down what they saw. One of these was a priest called Edward Grim, who just happened to be in the Cathedral on the day of the murder. Here is his account:

'Before long the butchers returned, wearing full armour and with swords and other weapons ready for their crime. The doors to the monastery grounds were locked, so they went down a side path and hacked their way through a wooden screen.

When they heard this terrible noise, the frightened priests and servants ran away like sheep before wolves.

Those who stayed shouted to the archbishop that he must run to the Cathedral church, but he would not go. Monks pleaded with him to go, and finally seized him and pushed him into the church.

The four knights ran quickly behind them. The wicked men entered the church, with drawn swords and noisy armour.

In a mad rage, one knight shouted, "Where is Thomas Becket, traitor to the king and the country?" Without any fear, Thomas walked down the steps to the knights, and answered in a clear voice, "Here I am. I am no traitor to the king but a priest of God. What do you want from me?" "Forgive those that you have condemned", a knight said. "I will not", replied the archbishop. "Then you shall die now and get what you deserve." "I am ready to die for my Lord God, that through my blood the Church should win peace and freedom."

Then they rushed at him, trying to drag him out of the church either to kill him or to carry him away as a prisoner, as they said themselves later. But Thomas held on to a pillar and would not let go.

One of the knights, Reginald Fitzurse, leapt on him and cut him on the top of the head. With the same stroke he almost cut off my arm. For, when the monks had run away, I had stood by the saintly archbishop and put my arms around him until one arm was nearly chopped off.

Becket was struck a second and third time and he fell to his knees murmuring, "For the name of Jesus and the protection of the Church, I am ready to die."

Richard Brito gave him a terrible blow as he lay on the floor. Hugh of Morville beat back anyone who tried to interfere. Hugh Mauclerc put his foot on the neck of the holy priest and, horrible to say, he scattered blood and brains across the floor calling to the others, "Let us go. This fellow will not be getting up again".'

Edward Grim, early 1170s

Source B gives a good impression of how Thomas Becket died. It also gives some clues as to why he was killed. Can you find any evidence in the source that:

a Thomas could have escaped death, but he seems to have wanted to be killed

b it is possible that the knights only wanted to arrest Becket but they lost their temper?

Can you see any other clues in the extract as to why Becket was killed?

Short-term and long-term causes

The causes of Becket's death which Edward Grim described would be called 'short-term' causes by historians. This means that the causes were developments that happened in a short time, perhaps a few weeks, before the event. Historians also look for 'long-term' causes; these have usually been building up over a long time, often a number of years.

Look at the following information about Becket. The order of the events has been deliberately jumbled up. For each development, work out whether you think it was a short-term or a long-term cause. Remember, Becket was killed on 29 December 1170.

a   On Christmas Day 1170, Henry II got very angry when he heard about what Becket had been doing. He said to his knights, 'You are cowards for letting this priest treat me so badly'. The knights who killed Becket then made a secret plan to go to Canterbury to show the king that they were not cowards.

b   The kings of England and archbishops of Canterbury had argued many times before Becket became archbishop. Each king wanted to show that he was in charge of everybody in the country, including priests and bishops. Each archbishop thought it was his job to make sure that the government did not take any power from the Church.

c   Becket arrived in England from France in early December 1170. He wanted everyone to know that he was still in charge of the Church. He 'excommunicated', or expelled, some bishops who had recently helped the king without asking for his permission as archbishop. Becket knew this would annoy the king.

d   King Henry II made Becket archbishop in 1162. Almost immediately they started to argue. Henry was angry because Becket had once been his close friend but would not help him after he had become archbishop. Becket was angry because Henry tried to change the law so that priests who had committed crimes did not get special treatment. Their arguments got so fierce that Becket had to leave the country in 1164 and live in France for six years.

e   The leader of the Catholic Church throughout Europe was the Pope. For a century before the death of Becket, popes had been saying that kings did not have power over the Church. This led to frequent disputes in many countries in Europe, including England.

SOURCE C
King Henry II. This picture was painted after Henry's death, in about 1250.

Saint Thomas

Becket had a sort of revenge for his murder after his death. He was made into a saint, and the scene of his death became a great pilgrimage centre. Henry apologised to the Church and allowed himself to be flogged by the monks of Canterbury – this was tremendous humiliation for a king.

---

1 You are a monk or nun in the year 1200, writing a chronicle for your abbey. You want to write a short paragraph about Becket's murder. Using Sources A and B, describe how Becket was killed.

2 Look at the different causes of Becket's death. Explain which ones were short-term and which ones were long-term.

3 Which do you think were more important, the short-term causes or the long-term causes?

4 Work in pairs. One of you should explain why Becket was a great man; the other why he was a fool. Find the differences in your opinions. What are they?

Bad King John?

For a long time people have disagreed about King John, who ruled England in the thirteenth century. Historians used to talk about 'Bad King John'.

Was John a bad King?

Thirteenth-century views of John

Look at these two descriptions written shortly after the death of King John.

SOURCE A

'John was a wicked ruler and not a proper king. He was a greedy money-grabber. Hell is too good for a foul person like him.'

Matthew Paris, thirteenth century

SOURCE B

'John was a great king, but he was not always successful. In part, this was because he was unlucky.'

Anonymous writer of the *Barnwell Chronicle*, thirteenth century

People at the time could not agree about King John. Historians have continued to disagree about John for centuries. What do you think he was like as a king?

Fighting in France

When John became king in 1199, he owned nearly as much land in France as in England. By 1204 John had lost much of his French territory, including Normandy. This was partly the fault of Richard the Lionheart, who was the king before John. Richard had made his nobles in France angry because he took so much money from them and many of them were tired of being ruled by an English king. Some of these nobles thought that a man called Arthur of Brittany would be a better ruler for them than John.

John loses Normandy

The people in France who did not like the idea of John as their new ruler soon went to war against him. At first things went well for John in this struggle and he captured many of his enemies, including Arthur of Brittany.

SOURCE C

One chronicle gives a full account of what happened to Arthur of Brittany.

'1203 After King John had captured Arthur and kept him in prison for a long time, he was moved to the castle at Rouen. After dinner one day when John was drunk and full of the devil, he killed Arthur by his own hand. Arthur's body was tied to a large stone and thrown into the river.'

Margam Chronicle, thirteenth century

After the death of Arthur, the war began to go badly for John. By 1204 he had to abandon Normandy and was forced to flee back to England.

A bitter struggle with the Pope

Like his father, Henry II, John spent a lot of his time arguing with Church leaders about how far the king should be able to tell the Church what to do. It was unfortunate for John that the Pope of the time, Innocent III, was very strong-minded and thought that kings should do as he told them. When the archbishop of Canterbury died in 1205, King John and the Pope argued about who should get the job next. Both men were stubborn, and neither would give way. After three years of angry disagreement the Pope decided to take action. In 1208 he ordered all clergymen in England to stop work.

SOURCE D

'1208 On 24 March, by order of the Pope, church services were stopped throughout England. This caused great unhappiness among the people. The bodies of the dead could not be buried in proper graveyards, so were placed in waste ground.'

Gervase of Canterbury, early thirteenth-century writer

The church strike went on from 1208 to 1213. In an age when nearly everybody believed in Christianity, and usually went to church, it was very upsetting for most people that the churches were shut for over five years. John was not very religious and does not seem to have been very bothered about the closed churches. In the end he decided to make his peace with Pope Innocent only because he thought the Pope might be able to help him in his fight with the barons.

Trouble with the barons

King John never really got over losing Normandy. He tried very hard to get his lands back, but by doing so he annoyed his great nobles or 'barons' back in England. He wanted to get more money from them to pay for more fighting, and he wanted them to cross over the Channel and help him personally in his wars. Most of the barons had no wish to part with more money or to fight in France.

In 1205 John met with his barons and tried to get them to come and fight with him to regain his lands in France.

After losing Normandy, John began to distrust his barons. He gave more and more important jobs to poor foreigners because he thought that they would be grateful to him and would not let him down. The barons expected to get the best jobs, so this made them even more unhappy with John.

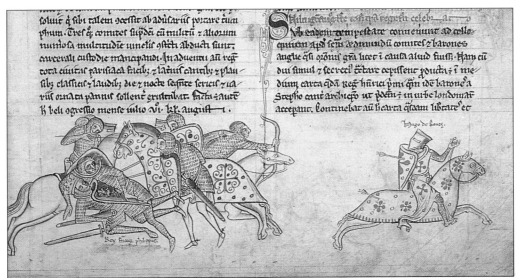

SOURCE E

John's soldiers fighting in France, 1214. What problems were caused when he tried to get his French lands back?

22

More money from the barons

John kept on trying to get back his lands in France all through his life. He tried to get as much money as possible from people in England, including the barons, to pay for armies. He charged heavy taxes. If he did not like a baron he would fine him, even if the baron had not broken any laws. When a baron took over from his father, he had to pay a special tax, called a 'relief'. As a result of all these payments, many barons were in debt.

> **SOURCE F**
>
> '1208 No one could stop the king from doing exactly what he wanted. He seemed to be the only powerful person in the country, and he was not afraid of God or any man.'
>
> Gervase of Canterbury, early thirteenth century

The barons rebel

In 1215 many of the English barons rebelled against John. The king had imposed a heavy new tax. The barons refused to pay, and they formed an army to fight the king. The rebel barons captured London and forced King John to sign a treaty in which he agreed to lots of their demands. This agreement was known as Magna Carta (The Great Charter). The agreement did not bring permanent peace. John was fighting again with the barons in 1216 when he died.

The meaning of Magna Carta

Over the years, many people have disagreed about Magna Carta. Some say that the barons were fighting for freedom and the rights of ordinary people against an unfair king. Others say that the barons were just being selfish and were fighting for their own interests. Look at the following extracts from Magna Carta and decide for yourself about the motives of the barons.

> **SOURCE G**
>
> ☆ the English Church shall be free and able to choose its own bishops without the king interfering
>
> ☆ if any baron dies, his heir should not have to pay more than £100 as a relief
>
> ☆ no special taxes should be imposed unless the barons meet and agree to it
>
> ☆ barons should not be fined unless they have committed an offence and are given a proper trial
>
> ☆ ordinary freemen should only be imprisoned if they have had a proper trial
>
> ☆ all hostages should be returned
>
> ☆ the barons shall choose twenty-five barons to check that the king does not break these rules
>
> Magna Carta, 1215

---

1 Work with a partner. Read Sources A and B. Decide for each of these events in John's life whether it shows that he was wicked or unlucky:

	Wicked?	Unlucky?
He lost lands in France		
He killed Arthur of Brittany		
He argued with the Pope		
He quarrelled with the barons		

2 Do the information and the sources in this unit suggest to you that John was wicked or just unlucky?

3 Why do you think people have had different opinions of King John, both while he was alive, and today?

4 Look at Source G. Do you think that Magna Carta shows that the barons were fighting for freedom and the rights of other people, or were they just being selfish?

England and the Celtic lands

Before 1066, the English had very little power over the Welsh and the Scots, and none at all over the Irish. This soon began to change after the Norman take-over. The Normans were greedy for more land. Soon they turned their attention beyond England, to the rest of the British Isles.

How successful were English attempts to take over the whole of the British Isles?

Overlord of Scotland

At the time of the Conquest, the Scots had their own king, Malcolm Canmore. He was in firm charge of the south and east of Scotland.

William the Conqueror did not try to take Scotland from Malcolm, but he did force Malcolm to agree that the king of England was overlord of the king of Scotland. To show that he was the more powerful, William marched an army through Scotland in 1072.

The Welsh – a divided people

The Welsh were divided in 1066. Unlike the Scots, they did not have a single king that all Welsh people could look to as leader. Rival families of princes ruled the different areas of Wales. This made it easier for the Normans to attack the Welsh. By 1100, the Normans had conquered a large slice of east and south Wales. Only in the mountains of the centre and the north were the Welsh princes able to keep out the Normans.

The Welsh fight back

In the early thirteenth century the Welsh started to fight back against the English. They were led by the princes of Gwynedd in the north-east of the country. By 1240, Llywelyn the Great of Gwynedd had taken control of much of Wales. His work was carried on by his grandson, Llywelyn the Last. The English king, Henry III, had trouble at home and was not strong enough to stop the growing power of the prince of Gwynedd. In 1267, he agreed that Llywelyn had power over the whole country and could call himself the Prince of Wales.

Mixed fortunes under Edward I

The power of the Welsh princes was destroyed for good by Edward I, towards the end of the thirteenth century. Llywelyn the Last was killed in 1282. The whole of Wales was brought firmly under English control, and a series of strong castles was built to stop the Welsh from winning back their freedom. Edward I gave his baby son the title of 'Prince of Wales' to show that the English were in control.

● Who is the Prince of Wales today?

Edward then turned his attention to Scotland and tried to take complete charge of the Scottish government. Edward I was not as successful as he had been in Wales. The Scots fought back well and were still fighting when Edward died. His son, King Edward II, was beaten by the Scottish king, Robert Bruce, at the Battle of Bannockburn in 1314. Although the fighting dragged on for a few more years, the English had failed.

For the rest of the Middle Ages, Scotland remained a free country. In contrast, Wales was ruled from London in the fourteenth and fifteenth centuries, apart from the period 1400–10 when a man named Owain Glyndwr led a Welsh rebellion against the English.

Strongbow and the Irish

In the eleventh century, the Normans were happy to leave Ireland alone. Like the Welsh, the Irish lacked a single ruler – each area of Ireland had its own king. In 1170, a century after the Norman Conquest in England, a Norman baron took an army to Ireland. His name was Richard FitzGilbert de Clare, but he is better known by his nickname, Strongbow.

Within a year, Strongbow had taken Dublin, and he became the most powerful man in Ireland. In 1171, the English king, Henry II, crossed over to Ireland and declared that Ireland was part of his lands. Within a few years the English had seized land across most of Ireland.

Dwindling power in Ireland

English control over Ireland grew weaker and weaker after 1300. The families of the Normans who had conquered the country began to speak the Irish language and live in an Irish way. The English government was too busy with other problems to make the Irish obey them. By 1500 only a small area around Dublin was under the control of the king of England.

The growth of national identity

Today when England, Scotland, Wales and Ireland play at rugby there is a strong sense of 'national pride'. The crowd for each side likes to feel that their country is different, special and better than the opposition. We can see the beginning of these feelings of 'national identity' during the Middle Ages. Look at the following sources.

SOURCE A

Henry II once marched through south Wales. He spoke to an old Welsh man and asked him when the Welsh would give in and let the English be in charge. This is the old man's answer.

'This nation may be attacked, weakened and destroyed by yours and others, but it will never be totally beaten. No other nation or language, except the Welsh, should have this corner of the earth.'

Old man of Pencader, quoted by Giraldus Cambrensis in his *Description of Wales,* late twelfth century

---

SOURCE B

In 1320, after many years of fighting the English, a group of leading Scottish nobles sent a letter to the Pope. This became known as *The Declaration of Arbroath.*

'If our king gives in to the English, we will immediately get rid of him and name another king. As long as there are a hundred of us alive to fight, we will never surrender to the rule of the English. We are not fighting for fame or money but for our freedom.'

The Declaration of Arbroath, 1320

SOURCE C

English feelings that they were better than foreigners grew towards the end of the Middle Ages. From around the year 1500 we have descriptions, written by unknown Italians, of what it was like to be a foreigner in London.

'Foreigners are treated like dirt and often insulted. By day, they gave us dirty looks, at night they sometimes attacked us with kicks and sticks . . . The Scots are more handsome, but the English are great lovers of themselves. They think England is the best place in the world. If they see a good-looking foreigner, they say, "He looks English".'

Anonymous descriptions of the English, about 1500

SOURCE D

*A thirteenth-century map of Britain. Can you see 'Wallia'
and 'Scotia'? Compare it with the map on page 79 to see
how accurate it is.*

1 Draw a line down the middle of a blank page. Make this into a time-line from 1066 to 1500. On the left-hand side mark those changes which increased the power of England over the rest of the British Isles. On the right-hand side mark those changes which reduced English power.

2 How successful was England in its attempts to take over Wales, Scotland and Ireland?

3 What were the feelings of national identity which started in the Middle Ages? Are today's feelings the same?

8

Bannockburn

In 1314 the Scots, led by Robert Bruce, defeated the English army of Edward II at the Battle of Bannockburn. This was one of the most important battles in medieval British history. If the English had won, Scotland would have been taken over and ruled from London. The defeat of Edward meant that Scotland could remain a separate state for many centuries.

Why did the Scots win at Bannockburn?

SOURCE A
Robert Bruce of Scotland: the victor

SOURCE B
King Edward II of England: defeated

Years of guerrilla warfare

For more than twenty years before Bannockburn the English had been trying to take over control of Scotland. Many Scots were ready to fight to stop the English, and from 1306 they were led by a tough new king, called Robert Bruce.

When Bruce became king he seemed to have little chance of winning, because the English army was bigger and stronger, and most Scottish castles were held by the English. Bruce was clever and he decided to fight a guerrilla war against the English. He avoided big battles, but used small-scale surprise attacks to destroy the power of the English slowly. These methods worked, and by early 1314 the English had lost nearly all of the Scottish castles. In that year, the English king, Edward II, decided that the time had come to smash Bruce and to take over Scotland once and for all.

The English march north

Edward's plan was to gather a huge army at Berwick-upon-Tweed and then march to Stirling Castle, which was still held by English soldiers. With Stirling as his base he could then begin to conquer the whole of Scotland. An impressive English army soon left Berwick with about 2,000 cavalry on horseback and a large number of foot-soldiers.

Bruce soon heard of Edward's plan and he got his own army ready to ambush the English. Unlike the English, the Scottish army had very few horsemen and was mostly made up of foot-soldiers.

The Scots take up position

The Scottish army was blocking the road to Stirling. Bruce stationed his soldiers at a place called New

Park, where the road passed through a forest. He chose New Park because the trees would make it easy to ambush the English. The only other way for the English to get to Stirling was to leave the road and try to cross some marshland. Many streams crossed the marshland, and the biggest of these was called the Bannock Burn.

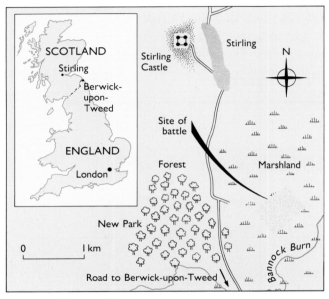

A map of Bannockburn.

The two armies meet

The English army reached New Park on 23 June 1314. Although they knew that Bruce was waiting, they did not think that there would be a big battle. The English leaders thought that Bruce would run away when he saw how large their army was.

First blood

Part of the English cavalry charged up to the forest. Robert Bruce was there in front of his own men. An English knight, Henry de Bohun, spotted Bruce and decided to try to kill him. Pointing his lance at Bruce, de Bohun galloped towards the Scottish king. If de Bohun had killed Bruce, the outcome of the battle and the future of Scotland could have been very different, but Bruce pulled his horse out of the way and de Bohun missed. As de Bohun rode past, Bruce stood up in his stirrups and smashed the

English knight's head in two with his battleaxe. The Scottish troops were very encouraged to see their king victorious and they charged at the rest of the English and forced them to retreat.

● What might have happened if de Bohun had killed Bruce?

A wall of men

A second group of English horsemen set out across the marshland to get round the back of the Scots. They were led by Sir Robert Clifford. He wanted to ride all the way round the New Park to stop the Scots from escaping by running away. Bruce sent out a party of Scottish foot-soldiers to meet the English cavalry. The Scots formed a tight wall of men, each one armed with a spear. The English cavalry tried to break through the wall, but many of their horses were killed by the spears and the survivors retreated. By now it was getting dark, and both sides decided to rest for the night.

SOURCE C
This account of how the English spent the night was written by a man whose father was in the English army.

'The English army left the road and crossed over the Bannock Burn onto an evil deep marsh, full of streams. There the English unharnessed their horses. They spent the night in discomfort, thinking about how things had gone badly for them on the previous day.'

Thomas Grey, fourteenth century

An English deserter

Although the Scots had done well on the first day of the battle, some of their leaders wanted to avoid any more fighting because they thought that they might lose. During the night, one member of the English army changed sides. His name was Alexander Seton, and he secretly made his way to the Scottish camp and spoke to Bruce.

SOURCE D

'My lord king, now is the time, if you ever want to win Scotland. The English have given up; they are uncomfortable and they expect defeat. You can hang me if I am wrong, but I say if you attack them in the morning, you will defeat them easily.'

The words of Alexander Seton according to Thomas Grey, fourteenth century

The second day of fighting

The Scottish army marched out of the forest of New Park and across towards Bannock Burn. The English king, Edward II, was amazed because he thought that the Scots did not want a big battle. Edward made a big mistake – he had his cavalry at the front and his archers at the back. If the archers had been at the front they could have sent waves of deadly arrows into the rows of Scottish foot-soldiers. As Edward tried to move his archers to the front, Bruce attacked them with his own small group of horsemen and he forced them to run away. The main body of Scottish foot-soldiers then did battle with mounted English knights. As on the previous day, the Scots formed a tight wall so that the English horsemen could not break through.

Edward II turned a difficult position into a complete disaster by deciding to leave the battle. As word spread among the English that their king was retreating, they gave up hope and tried to escape. Many of the English knights could not get their heavy horses across the Bannock Burn to safety. Those who could not get away were killed or drowned. The Scots had won.

SOURCE E

At Bannockburn foot-soldiers got the better of the mounted knights. This picture comes from a French manuscript of about 1250.

1 Research these events from the unit and discuss why they made a difference to the battle:

♦ Bruce was an experienced soldier
♦ Bruce put his army in a good position
♦ the English were badly organised
♦ Bruce killed de Bohun
♦ Scottish foot-soldiers were able to kill the horses of the English
♦ the English had to sleep in the middle of a marsh
♦ Seton changed sides
♦ the English archers were in the wrong place
♦ Edward II ran away.

2 For each event discuss whether you think it was a major or a minor reason for the Scottish victory.

3 Work with a partner. Imagine that you are producing a history of Scotland for seven- to eight-year-olds. Tell the story of Bannockburn in the form of a two-page cartoon strip. The aim of the cartoon is to explain to these young children why Robert Bruce won the battle. Think carefully about which reasons you choose.

9

The Peasants' Revolt of 1381

For most of the Middle Ages, ordinary people played little part in politics. They had no votes and no power: rich people made all the important decisions. Kings could ignore what poor people wanted. For a few weeks in 1381 all this changed. A huge army of poor people marched to London. They killed many rich people and complained to King Richard II.

Why did so many ordinary people rise up in the Peasants' Revolt?

Trouble with landlords

Throughout the Middle Ages there were arguments between poor serfs (peasants who were not free) and their rich landlords. Serfs often thought that they were made to work too hard by their landlords. Sometimes this led to violence.

SOURCE A

'In 1336, the villagers of Demhale and Over complained that they should really be free. A great crowd met their lord, the abbot, on the highway, where they attacked and killed his groom, William Finch. The abbot put them all in chains to show that they were his slaves.'

The Ledger Book of Vale Royal Abbey, fourteenth century

The tension gets worse

There was an increase in unrest after the Black Death of 1349. So many people died of the disease that there was a great shortage of workers. This encouraged the surviving workers to demand better conditions. The king and the great lords were unhappy at this and they passed a new law saying that no one should be paid any more than they were before the Black Death. The law also said that anyone who refused to work would be put in prison.

SOURCE B

Judges were sent round the country to make sure that the new law was obeyed.

'Many of these judges were attacked in the Peasants' Revolt of 1381. It cannot be a coincidence that more violence took place in those counties where the judges were most active.'

B Dobson, *The Peasants' Revolt of 1381,* 1970

SOURCE C
John Ball leading the Peasants' Revolt. From a fourteenth-century manuscript.

The preaching of poor priests

Although bishops and abbots were often rich, there were many poor priests in the fourteenth century. Some of these seem to have preached a message of rebellion. The most famous poor priest was John Ball, and he became one of the leaders of the Peasants' Revolt.

The final straw

The Peasants' Revolt started in Essex during May 1381. Special tax-collectors and judges had been sent to the county because some people were refusing to pay a new government poll tax. It was the third time in four years that the government had demanded that people pay extra taxes.

SOURCE E

Handing over tax to the government. What part did this play in the Revolt? From the 'Canterbury Psalter', a twelfth-century manuscript.

Rebellion soon broke out in Kent. The people of Kent marched to Maidstone, where they beheaded one of the richest men in the town. They made Wat Tyler of Maidstone their leader.

On 12 June the rebels of Kent came to Blackheath, near London, and the people of Essex arrived on the other side of the river.

The Revolt reaches London

Some of the people inside London seem to have supported the rebels – the gates of the city were opened and the mob entered. Once inside, they burned down the houses of members of the government and of foreigners. King Richard and his chief ministers fled for safety to the Tower of London.

On Friday 14 June, King Richard left the Tower and went to meet some of the rebels at a place called Mile End. The people complained at how badly treated they were as serfs. To keep them quiet, the king gave them a document declaring that all men in England were free, and that never again should anyone have to be a serf.

While King Richard was at Mile End, another band of rebels broke into the Tower of London.

Showdown at Smithfield

On the next day, Saturday 15 June, King Richard went out to meet the rebels at Smithfield Market. Wat Tyler rode up to talk to the king. Tyler insulted the king by spitting in front of him, and pulling out a knife to threaten one of the king's knights.

The king ordered the mayor of London to arrest Tyler. The mayor struck Tyler on the head and badly injured him. Other friends of the king surrounded Tyler. They finished him off with their swords, and Tyler fell dead from his horse.

When they saw what had happened, the rest of the people got ready to shoot with their arrows, but the king rode towards them and said, 'What are you doing? Don't shoot at your own king. I will be your new leader. Follow me into the next field and we can talk about all your complaints.' When they heard this, the people followed the king.

The collapse of the Revolt

While the king played for time by talking to the rebels, the mayor of London went to get reinforcements. He soon returned with a large force of armed men who surrounded the rebels. Seeing that they could be killed, the rebels threw down their weapons and surrendered. They knelt down and begged the king not to kill them. The king ordered the rebels to go home immediately – any rebel found in London that night would be executed.

The main part of the Peasants' Revolt was over. There were also serious outbreaks of violence as far north as Chester and York. Once peace was restored, the government started to punish the rebels. All the promises of freedom made during the Revolt were cancelled. The leaders of the rebels were captured and executed.

Different causes of the Revolt. Find three more causes to add to the one already completed.

---

1 How can we tell from Source A that landlords and their serfs had been getting on badly for many years before the Peasants' Revolt of 1381?

2 Why did the Black Death increase bad feelings between workers and the great lords?

3 Look at Source D. In what way did poor priests like John Ball encourage serfs to rebel?

4 Using the information in this unit, explain why each of the people shown in the cartoon went to see King Richard.

5 Write your own eye-witness account of the death of Wat Tyler. You can be for or against him. Compare your account with that of a friend.

Richard III: hero or villain?

> Richard III was king of England from 1483 to 1485. Although his reign was very short, he created a very powerful impression on people at the time. For many centuries people have disagreed very strongly about Richard.
>
> *What sort of king was Richard III?*

SOURCE A

'He was the most terrifying man ever to be the king of England. His short life was filled with intrigue and he was guilty of slaughtering other people.'

D Seward, *Richard III: England's Black Legend*, 1983

SOURCE B

'He was almost a model English king. He was a great soldier. He was generous to the Church, and he was a champion of justice.'

M Bennett, *The Battle of Bosworth*, 1985

Clearly Sources A and B disagree. Your task in this unit is to try to work out which view is correct.

Richard's early career

Richard was the brother of Edward IV, who was king from 1461 to 1483. While his brother was alive, Richard was known as the Duke of Gloucester. He spent much of his time in the north of England, where he owned a lot of land. He was popular there and won the respect of the local people.

Uncle Richard helps out

Edward IV died unexpectedly on 9 April 1483. He left two sons, Edward and Richard. They were both children. The oldest was named King Edward V

SOURCE C
King Richard III, painted by an unknown artist. What impression do you get from this painting?

after his father's death. He was too young to rule, so his uncle Richard said that he would look after the country until Edward was old enough. Richard marched to Northamptonshire and seized the young king.

The widow of Edward IV, Queen Elizabeth, did not trust Richard, and she went with her younger son to Westminster Abbey, where she thought they would be safe. Richard surrounded the building with his troops and forced the queen to surrender her son.

Richard seizes the crown

At first, Richard announced that Edward V would soon be crowned king. By the end of June 1483, he was saying something very different. He claimed that Queen Elizabeth had not been properly married to Edward IV. This meant that her sons were illegitimate and therefore had no claim to the throne.

SOURCE D

'Richard brought armed men in frightening numbers to London from the North. On 26 June he claimed that he was the new king, and he sat in the marble throne at Westminster.'

Anonymous, *Chronicle of Crowland Abbey,* 1486

What happened to the princes in the Tower?

The two young princes, Edward and Richard, were sent by their uncle to the Tower of London. After July 1483 they mysteriously disappeared and were never seen again.

SOURCE E

A modern historian writes:

'No one will ever know when, or even whether, Richard III had his nephews murdered in the Tower of London.'

K Dockray, *Richard III,* 1988

On 17 July 1674 some men were digging in the Tower. They found the bones of two youngsters in a wooden box about ten feet underground. They seemed to be about thirteen and eleven years old. No one has been able to prove who these skeletons were.

● What do you think happened to the princes?

Richard as ruler

What sort of government did Richard provide during his short reign?

SOURCE F

'The king is determined to see good justice throughout the kingdom, and to punish all who break the law. For this reason, he wishes that during his visit to Kent all people of that county with a complaint should put it to the king, and the matter shall be dealt with.'

Royal Proclamation to Kent, 1483

SOURCE G

'King Richard deserves praise for his building of the churches of Westminster, Nottingham, Warwick, York and Middleham and many other places. He gave Queens' College, Cambridge over £300 a year. The people of London, Gloucester and Worcester offered him money but he returned it saying that he would rather have their love than their money.'

John Rous, *History of the Kings of England,* 1491

SOURCE H

A nineteenth-century view of the princes in the Tower. What did the artist, Delaroche, think about the princes?

Death at Bosworth

Richard III was killed at the Battle of Bosworth Field in August 1485. The battle was very important because it marked the end of the Wars of the Roses. The winning army was led by Henry Tudor. Henry became the first Tudor king of England.

Many of Richard's supporters changed sides and joined Henry before and during the battle.

SOURCE I

Fighting in the late fifteenth century. This picture was painted in about 1470.

SOURCE J

'They say that King Richard could have saved himself by running away. His friends, seeing how badly his soldiers fought and that some were disappearing, urged him to go and brought him swift horses. He answered that he would win or die.'

Polydore Vergil, *English History*, early sixteenth century

● What can we learn about Richard from the way he behaved at Bosworth?

---

1 Explain how Sources A and B disagree about what sort of man Richard III was.

2 What information can you find in the rest of the unit that supports the views of Source A?

3 What information can you find in the rest of the unit that supports the views of Source B?

4 How do you think it is possible for historians to come to such different conclusions?

5 Imagine that the government has set up an inquiry to settle the question of whether Richard was a terrible king or a great king. You are in charge of the enquiry. Produce a report that explains your views.

A chronicle of

1086 The Normans put together the Domesday Book

Twenty years after invading, William the Conqueror ordered a great survey of his new lands. It became known as the Domesday Book. The Normans used it to work out how much tax they could get from different areas. The Domesday Book showed a picture of a land where most people worked in the countryside and towns were very small.

1100 The Normans encourage new towns wherever they go

There was a great increase in the number and size of towns after the Norman Conquest. Many were market towns where local farmers came to buy and sell. Some towns had castles and courts, and were used to govern the local area. Then, as now, London was far bigger than all the other towns.

1066–1300 There is a great increase in the population

The two centuries after the Conquest saw more and more people living in the British Isles. Areas of forest and waste land were ploughed up to get more food. Some of this new farm land was very poor and did not produce good crops.

1300–50 Farming goes through a great crisis

By 1300 there were too many people in the countryside. Not enough food could be produced to keep them healthy. Bad weather spoiled many harvests. Large numbers of sheep and cattle died from animal diseases.

economic changes

The bubonic plague, or 'Black Death', arrived in Britain in 1348. Although we have no exact figures, it seems that about one in three of all people died. The plague returned in following years to kill more. In this terrible way the problem of the over-crowded countryside was solved.

1348–49 The Black Death kills about a third of the population

With a smaller population, farms and whole villages were deserted over a number of years. Some of the land that had been used for crops was changed to grazing for animals, especially sheep, but there was still enough land to grow crops because there were fewer people.

1300–1500 Many villages are deserted

A smaller population meant less trade for some towns in the late Middle Ages. Some went through a bad time with abandoned shops and houses. Other towns, especially those involved in the wool trade, did well. London continued to grow.

1350–1500 Towns have very mixed fortunes

Ordinary working people did better after the Black Death. There was a shortage of workers so they were able to get higher wages. It was easier for farmers to get bigger farms and become richer.

1350–1500 Ordinary people are better off

11

The countryside

When William conquered England in 1066, he claimed all the land in the country was his own property. He introduced a new system of organising it.

How was the land organised during the Middle Ages?

A system called feudalism. Each person who receives land gives something in exchange.

Feudalism

William agreed to give much of the land to a few noblemen and to the leaders of the Church. These people were called the 'tenants-in-chief'. He kept about 20 per cent of all the land for himself, and gave the remaining 80 per cent to about 180 tenants-in-chief.

In return for these huge amounts of land, the tenants-in-chief agreed to provide William with soldiers when he needed them. The tenants-in-chief themselves divided up their land and gave it to a number of knights. The knights in return agreed to fight when they were needed. This exchange of land for soldiers was called the 'feudal system'.

SOURCE A

'Knights have their lands in return for military service. They should not have to pay any rents or taxes for their lands. In return, they should be equipped with a coat of mail, and enough horses and weapons, so that they can defend the kingdom.'

The Coronation Oath of Henry I, 1100

A solemn bond

The feudal system was more than a simple deal over farmland and soldiers. The king, the barons (as the tenants-in-chief were often called) and the knights made a lifelong promise to look after each other.

Letting someone down was a great disgrace. The Normans took the feudal system into some of the lands they conquered in Wales and Ireland, and feudal ideas spread into parts of Scotland.

SOURCE B

A king and one of his tenants-in-chief. From a late fourteenth-century manuscript.

Strips of land

Farming in medieval Britain varied a lot from place to place. In central and southern England, the 'open field system' was most common. How did the open field system work?

Most of the land of a village was divided into two huge fields. Inside each big field were a large number of long, thin 'strips' of land. Any one farming family would have a number of strips scattered across all the big fields. The longest strips were a furlong in length (about 200 metres), and about eight metres wide. A furlong was approximately the distance that an ox team could plough before resting.

At any one time, one of the open fields would be growing crops like wheat, barley, oats or beans. The other one would be left 'fallow', with no crops at all. The fallow land was allowed to rest and regain its goodness. Animals were grazed on the fallow field, fertilising it with their manure. The fallow field would change, or rotate, each year.

The whole village shared the pasture land outside the open fields. This land was also used for keeping animals.

● How does this system compare with farming today? Do farmers in Britain still grow their crops in narrow strips? Does it vary in different parts of the country?

Problems for the farmers

If it was to work properly, the open field system needed the whole village to co-operate. There were no fences between the strips, and this sometimes led to arguments.

SOURCE C

A photograph taken from the air of the deserted medieval village of Middle Ditchford in Gloucestershire. From photographs like this we can see the layout of the village and the strips in the fields.

An artist's reconstruction of what the village of Middle Ditchford may have looked like.

39

SOURCE D

Sowing corn in the mid-fourteenth century. What problems did farmers like this face at the time?

SOURCE E

'Richard of Ashton complains that Nicholas of the Wood wickedly moved the boundary between their lands. For this Richard of Ashton must pay damages of £1 and a fine of 10s. [50p].'

The Court Baron, a thirteenth-century lawyers' textbook

SOURCE F

A poet put these words into the mouth of a farmer.

'When I went ploughing I tried to pinch a foot of land from my neighbour. If I was reaping, I would reach into my neighbour's strip and take with my sickle crops that I had not sown.'

William Langland, *Piers Plowman*, fourteenth century

● What other difficulties do you think were caused by farming in narrow strips?

● Were there any advantages in the open field system? Think about the quality of the land – would it all be equally good?

SOURCE G

Serfs working on the land of their lord. They are harvesting with sickles. The bailiff (estate manager) is checking their work carefully. From a thirteenth-century calendar.

The open fields caused other problems, too. A family with a large holding of thirty acres could have their land scattered across the two big fields in more than sixty separate strips. Simply moving from strip to strip could waste a lot of time.

All the farmers had to agree on the dates for ploughing, sowing and harvesting. They had to share their ploughs. It was very difficult for individual farmers to experiment.

40

Farming in other areas of Britain

There were many areas that did not have the open fields of central and southern England. Look at these sources and try to work out why the system was not used everywhere.

SOURCE H

'Many parts of northern England are barren and cannot grow cereal crops, especially wheat. But these areas are rich in animals and fish. The locals enjoy lots of milk and butter and the rich people have lots of meat.'

William of Malmesbury, early twelfth century

SOURCE I

'In Ireland the fields are usually used for pasturing animals. Few crops are grown. In Wales the greater part of the land is used for pasture. They grow very little and do not sow much seed.'

Giraldus Cambrensis, late twelfth century

More mouths to feed

There were many small towns in medieval Britain, but the great majority of people lived in the countryside. Although it is difficult to be accurate, historians now think that at the time of Domesday, the population of England was about two million. It increased very sharply in the following two centuries. By 1300 there may have been as many as seven million people. In order to grow more food for all these people, villagers divided the two fields into three and tried to plough poorer land.

Disaster for the farmers

The countryside went through a great crisis in the fourteenth century. There were too many people. Much of the land being used was so poor that it yielded very small crops. The temperature became a little colder, and some harvests were ruined by heavy rains. The final straw was the coming of the plague of 1348–49, that killed over a third of the population. The plague came back in 1361 and 1368 to kill more. As a result of all these problems, many villages were gradually abandoned, and people gave up trying to grow crops on the poorest soils. By the fifteenth century, less land was ploughed, and much more was used for animal pasture, especially for grazing sheep.

---

1 In your own words, explain how the open field system worked. What were the open fields? How many were there in a village? How were they divided up?

2 What happened when fields were left fallow?

3 Why did the open field system require lots of co-operation between neighbours?

4 What can we learn from Sources E and F about some of the problems of the open fields?

5 Look at Sources H and I. Why do you think the open field system was not found everywhere?

6 Many people think villages were abandoned because the landlords forced the villagers to leave so they could graze sheep and make good profits. How accurate is this idea?

12

Work without pay

Serfs were not free. They were their landlord's property. They had to stay in the same village for the whole of their lives. They had to work very hard, but was life unbearable for them?

How well did the rich landlords treat their workers?

A life of restrictions

The ordinary men and women of the countryside were either free or unfree. Free peasants simply paid rent to the lord for their land. The unfree were called serfs.

Serfs not only had to pay a rent, they also had to do a number of services for their lord. The heaviest of these services was having to work a number of days a week on the lord's land for no pay. Although it varied from place to place, typical serfs might have to work three days a week for their lord, and could only work on their own land on the remaining days. At harvest time, the number of days of service was often increased.

Other restrictions on serfs:
★ a lord could charge the serfs on his land a number of different taxes
★ when serfs took over some land, they paid a tax called a 'relief' to the lord
★ when serfs died, their family had to give the lord the best animal in a tax called 'heriot'
★ they had to make a special payment called 'merchet' to get permission to marry
★ they could not leave the village without permission.

Look at the following sources and think about the good and bad sides of life in a medieval village.

SOURCE A

'We are called their slaves, and unless we do as we are told we get beaten.'

John Ball, a poor priest, preaching during the Peasants' Revolt, 1381

SOURCE B

'A bailiff should be with the workers at all times to see that they are working properly, and at the end of the day should check on how much they have done. Serfs do not work well and you must check to stop them stealing. If they do not work hard they should be punished.'

Walter of Henley, *On Husbandry*, thirteenth century

SOURCE C

Some serfs were better off than others. A modern historian wrote this description of a serf with a lot of land.

'He would probably be married, and have sons and daughters, and even servants to help him. He was able to plough his own acres and those of his lord by the simple method of sending one or more of his own family to the manor house, while the rest carried on at home.'

H S Bennet, *Life on the English Manor*, 1937

SOURCE D

Villagers having a dance in their time off from work. From a fifteenth-century manuscript.

SOURCE E

This extract is written by a modern historian.

'The medieval peasant ate good wholemeal bread and was able to get 5,000 calories a day out of the bread. He did not need meat because he had good bread and dairy products, herrings, onions, leeks and garlic.'

H E Hallam, *Rural England 1066–1348*, 1981

● Find out whether 5,000 calories is enough for an adult who is doing hard physical work.

SOURCE F

'Every labourer must be at work in summer by 5 o'clock in the morning. He should have half an hour for breakfast, and an hour and a half off for dinner. He should not leave work until 7 o'clock in the evening. In winter he should work all the daylight hours.'

Royal Law, 1495

SOURCE G

This description of life inside a peasant's house was written by a fourteenth-century poet.

'Three things can drive a man to leave his house. The first is a wife who will not do as she is told. The second is a leaky roof so that it rains on his bed. The third and worst is the smoke from the fire that makes him blind, bleary-eyed and hoarse.'

William Langland, *Piers Plowman*, fourteenth century

SOURCE H

In some villages, the lord had the right to order serfs to marry particular people, or pay a fine.

'1279 Thomas Robins of Oldbury came and was commanded to take Agatha of Halesowen as his wife. He said that he would rather be fined.'

Halesowen Manor Records, thirteenth century

---

1 Divide your page in two. Look back at the sources and then make a list of all the bad things and all the good things about being a serf living in a medieval village.

2 How can you explain the fact that some of the sources show that it was terrible to be a serf, while others show that life could be pleasant?

3 Design a board game about the life of a serf. Make a track of a number of squares, and make some counters that look like serfs.

Find some dice. The final square should say 'You have run away and lived in a town for a year. This means you are now free'. The object of the game is get to this 'freedom' square first. Put some of the bad and good things about country life onto different squares. For example, 'Your lord takes some money from you because you want to get married, go back four squares'. Decorate the board with some suitable pictures.

13

Women in the countryside

Women played a vital role in the medieval countryside. Many of them worked hard at home and in the field.

How harsh was life for women in a medieval village?

SOURCE A

This description of the life of country women was written by a fourteenth-century poet.

'Charged with children and overcharged by landlords
What they may spare in spinning, they spend on rent.
On milk or on meal to make porridge
To still the sobbing of the children at meal times…
Also themselves suffer much hunger
And woe in wintertime, with waking at night
To rise to the [bedside] to rock the cradle…
The woe of these women who dwell in hovels is too sad to speak of or to say in rhyme.'

William Langland, *Piers Plowman*, fourteenth century

SOURCE B

The alehouse was an important feature in most villages. This is a women's drinking song.

'Call out our good friends by and by,
Eleanor, Joan and Margery,
Margaret, Alice and Cecily,
For they will come,
Both all and some.
And each of them will something bring,
Goose or pig or chicken wing,
Pasties of pigeon or some other thing,
For we must eat,
Some manner of meat.
If my husband might here see me,
A blow or two he will give me,
She who's frightened let her flee,
Said Alice then,
"I fear no man."'

Anonymous fifteenth-century song

● Was this typical for all women living in the countryside?

● How useful is a song as a piece of historical evidence?

SOURCE C

A country woman feeding a hen and chickens. She is carrying a distaff which was used for spinning woollen yarn. Why do you think she is carrying it? From a fourteeth-century manuscript.

SOURCE E

A lady defending herself and her household against attack. From a fifteenth-century manuscript.

SOURCE D

This extract is taken from a fourteenth-century poem.

'As I went along I saw a poor man ploughing. His wife walked beside him with a long stick for the oxen. She had a short dress on and had wrapped a sheet around herself to keep warm. She went barefoot on the frozen ground and her feet were bleeding. At the end of a field was a baby in rags and two 2-year-olds. The children cried all the time.'

Anonymous poem, fourteenth century

SOURCE F

Not all women in the village were involved in heavy physical work. In some villages the 'lord' was actually a lady. This happened in the case of some widows, and when the land belonged to a nunnery. Upper-class women often led busy lives running estates. One such example was the abbess of Chatteris in East Anglia.

'The village of Foxton pays the Lady 13s. 4d.[66p] for common aid [tax].
Richard Brun pays the Lady for permission for his daughter to marry Warin West.
Christiana Attgate pays 2s. [10p] for permission to marry an outsider.'

Records of the Nunnery of Chatteris, early fourteenth century.
Quoted in R Parker, *The Common Stream,* 1976

SOURCE G

'Servants and labourers will not work unless they receive outrageous wages. From now on wages shall be fixed at 13s. 4d. [66p] and his clothes once a year for a bailiff, 10s. [50p] a year for a foreman, 10s. [50p] a year for a shepherd, 7s. [35p] a year for a ploughman, 6s. [30p] a year for a woman labourer.'

Government Law, 1388

● What does this tell us about women's wages?

SOURCE H

'Thomas Cusin came to the house of Gunilda de Stokes, carried her out into the fields, and took away all her goods. She complained about Thomas to the king's judges. He said in court that he was entitled to take her goods and throw her out of her house because she was his serf. The court agreed with him and the case was dismissed.'

Court Records, 1244

SOURCE I

Eleanor, Countess of Leicester lived in the thirteenth century. Her household papers have survived and they give us some idea of the lifestyle of a wealthy, independent woman.

'On Sunday 26 April 1265, for a meal for the Countess and her guests, Master Richard the Chaplain of Kemsing and Master John, priest of Catherington, and members of her household, the following costs:

seven bushels [250 kilograms] of flour for bread
eleven gallons of wine and some ale
one and a half oxen and three sheep
some calves and hens
two small goats from the castle stores
150 eggs given as rent by the villagers
some milk.'

The Household Records of the Countess of Leicester, 1265

SOURCE J
A woman hunting a stag. Rich men and women enjoyed hunting wild animals. From an early fourteenth-century manuscript.

1 Look at Source B. What does it tell us about how some women spent their leisure time?

2 Can we learn anything from Source B about how men and women got on together?

3 Can you find any information from the other sources that:
a some women were very poor
b some women were very rich
c women were not treated fairly all the time
d some women had power over men?

4 How useful are the two pictures compared with the written sources for learning about women in the countryside?

5 'Women in the medieval countryside were badly treated.' Using all the sources in this unit, explain whether you agree or disagree with this statement.

The changing face of town life

Nowadays many more people live in towns than in the countryside. In the Middle Ages the opposite was true – over 90 per cent of the population lived in small country villages. The medieval towns were much smaller than modern cities. Nearly seven million people live in London today, but in 1150 its population was about 25,000.

How did towns change in the Middle Ages?

The towns grow

Towns grew in size between 1100 and 1300. There were also lots of completely new towns. Why was this?

The population of the whole country was growing at the time. Poor serfs from country villages often ran away to towns to seek a new life. When this happened, the lord of the village would usually try to find them and take them back to the village. But often they did not succeed.

SOURCE A

The town charter of Gloucester made it clear that the right of a lord to get his serf back was limited. Other towns had similar rules.

'If any serf of another man should stay in the town and support himself and pay his taxes for a year and a day, after that time he cannot be reclaimed by his lord.'

Royal Charter to Gloucester, 1227

Although most people lived and worked in the countryside, the local town was important to them as a place where they went to market. Between 1100 and 1300, more and more food was produced in the countryside, and this was another reason why so many towns grew at the time. In the market town the country people could sell their spare food for money. Here the better-off villagers could buy luxury goods from abroad like wine or cooking spices.

The rich burgesses take power

People who had the right to trade in towns were called 'burgesses'. In the eleventh century, people in the towns had little power; they had to obey the instructions of the king and local landowners. In the twelfth and thirteenth centuries, as towns grew bigger and richer, they won some freedom from the king and his nobles.

In many towns the rich traders formed an organisation called the 'Merchant Guild', which controlled business in the town. They would meet to make their decisions at an important building called 'The Guildhall'.

The workers organise

Ordinary workers in particular trades organised themselves into 'craft guilds'. After 1300, the craft guilds became important in the life of most towns. Brewers, bakers, weavers, tailors and many other traders had their own guild. The guilds kept a check on who was allowed to do work in the craft and on the quality of work. They also looked after members who became old or sick.

William the Conqueror visiting the town of Lincoln in 1068. A modern artist's impression.

Edward III visiting Lincoln in 1327. How had it changed since the time of William the Conqueror?

Guilds were divided into three. The trainees were called 'apprentices'. They were usually about twelve or thirteen years old, and they worked for their master for seven years to learn the trade. The full members of the guild were skilled workers, and were known as 'journeymen'. The senior members were called 'masters'.

● Can you find any similarities between guilds and the trade unions we have today?

Hard times

The population of many of the towns fell in the fourteenth century. Many people died of the plague; some of the shops and markets did much less business. In the twelfth century, the population of Winchester was about 7,000. By 1377 the population was down to 2,000. Not all towns went through a bad time. London continued to grow, and so did many of the towns such as Lavenham and Chipping Campden, which were involved in the wool trade.

London: a medieval city

London was much larger than any other town or city in medieval Britain.

● What was London like in medieval times?

SOURCE C

A man from London wrote this description.

'There are in London thirteen monasteries and 126 parish churches. Every week at Smithfield there is a well-known market for horses. Great noblemen and townsfolk come out to inspect and buy the horses. In another part of Smithfield country people sell their goods, farming equipment, large pigs, cows, oxen and woolly sheep. To this city come traders from all over the world. You can buy Arabian gold, precious jewels from Egypt, furs from Norway and Russia, silk from China and French wine.'

William Fitzstephen, about 1170

SOURCE D

Town courts often had to deal with matters of public health.

'Cases discussed at the court of Robert Chichele, mayor of the city of London:
- The master of Ludgate often puts dung out onto the street and blocks the water flowing in the gutter.
- The public lavatory of Ludgate is broken and dangerous and the filth from there is rotting the stone walls.'

London Court Records, 1422

SOURCE E

A medieval painting of a walled city.

SOURCE F

Some of the richest towns in the Middle Ages were in Italy, so it is interesting to find out what an Italian visitor thought of London.

'In one single street called The Strand, leading to St Paul's, there were fifty-two goldsmiths' shops, each one rich and full of goods. If you put all the shops of Milan, Rome, Venice and Florence together, I do not think you would find as many as magnificent as those in London.'

Unknown Italian writer, about 1500

1 What happened to the size of towns between 1100 and 1300?

2 What happened to the size of towns between 1300 and 1500?

3 What reasons can you find to explain these changes in the size of towns?

4 a What was the difference between a Merchant Guild and a craft guild?
b In what ways did people in towns become more powerful after 1200?

5 'All towns changed in the Middle Ages, but they changed in different ways.' Do you agree?

6 Look at Sources B and C. Do the writers agree about what sort of place London was?

7 Make two headings, 'Good points' and 'Bad points'. Use Source B–F to make two lists about medieval London . Why do you think the sources disagree so much?

8 Write your own description of medieval London in a few lines. Compare it with a friend's description and discuss your differences.

A chronicle of

Medicine in the Middle Ages was very different from what it is today. Doctors used astrology and studied the colour of their patients' urine to work out why they were ill. Surgery was very primitive. Only the rich could afford doctors – ordinary people used local healers, many of whom were women.

1066–1500 Only rich people can afford to use doctors

The number of monks and nuns increased after the Conquest. There were important new religious orders such as the Cistercians. Monasteries were given huge amounts of land by wealthy supporters. They became very rich, which made it difficult for their members to lead a simple life.

1066–1300 The religious orders grow larger and larger

Organising law and order was an important part of a king's work. Henry II brought in some major changes. He encouraged the idea of local juries to decide who was guilty. He also sent royal judges on regular trips across the country to deal with serious crimes.

1160 Henry II changes the court system

A new religious group called the friars came to Britain in the thirteenth century. They were different from monks and nuns because they worked and preached in towns, among ordinary people. The first friars were very proud of how poor they were.

1200–1300 The friars arrive

ideas and beliefs

In the early Middle Ages, Jews were the only non-Christians who were allowed to live in Britain. They often did useful work as bankers. Jews were badly treated and occasionally murdered by Christian mobs. The English king, Edward II, forced them to leave in 1290.

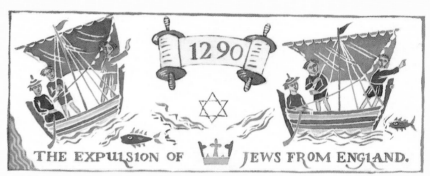

1290 Edward II forces the Jews to leave England

Throughout the Middle Ages the Church was Catholic. A fourteenth-century writer called John Wyclif said that Catholic teaching was wrong. He had followers known as Lollards. The government made being a Lollard a crime, and some of them were burned to death.

1380–1500 Lollards oppose the Catholic Church

Monasteries and nunneries remained rich and powerful until the end of the Middle Ages. However, men and women were less attracted to this way of life. Many monks and nuns began to break the strict rules they were supposed to keep.

1400–1500 Fewer people become monks and nuns

Most people believed firmly in Christianity. However, by the end of the Middle Ages, the priests were disliked by many, especially in the larger towns. They felt that the Church was more interested in making money than in teaching about Christ.

1400–1500 The Church becomes unpopular, especially in the towns

15

Law and order

In the later Middle Ages, as today, some people got into trouble with the law. However, the way they were treated was often very different from our modern system of justice.

What happened to criminals in the Middle Ages?

In the later Middle Ages the treatment of criminals was confused. There were lots of different types of law court, and it was not always clear which court should deal with which crime. The king's government had its own courts, but so did the Church and local landowners.

Trial by ordeal

Some methods which seem strange to us today were used in medieval times to find out if a person was guilty of a crime. If it was not clear from the evidence of witnesses that a person was guilty, the suspect had to go through a 'trial by ordeal'. In the ordeal by fire, the suspect was given a red hot iron bar and had to carry it for three paces. The hand was then bandaged. Three days later the bandage was removed – if a large blister had formed, the person was considered to be guilty. For a serious crime the guilty person would then be hanged.

SOURCE A
Early medieval punishment could be very severe.

'Death is the punishment for a thief caught in the act, whether Norman or English, if the criminal is more than twelve years old and the value of the property more than eight pence.'

Laws of Henry I, about 1100

Church law

SOURCE B
The same source shows that some people could get off very lightly. Members of the Church were given special treatment.

'If a priest kills a man he shall be deprived of his job and his position and shall go abroad on a pilgrimage.'

Laws of Henry I, about 1100

A new system: trial by jury

When Henry II became king of England in 1154, he decided to improve the court system. Regular royal courts were set up to deal with serious cases like robbery and murder. Judges were frequently sent round the country to hold trials. The jury became a common way of deciding a case – twelve trustworthy men from an area were asked to decide if someone was guilty of a crime.

After the time of Henry II, trial by ordeal became very rare and in the thirteenth century it stopped altogether. Henry was less successful in getting rid of the special treatment for members of the Church who had broken the law. His attempt to get rid of the light penalties for priests who were criminals led to his famous argument with Archbishop Thomas Becket. Henry did not win the argument and priests continued to be dealt with separately from other criminals.

SOURCE C

A travelling court like those set up by Henry II. This picture comes from a fifteenth-century manuscript.

Seeking sanctuary

Some strange traditions were not affected by Henry's changes. One of these was 'sanctuary'. If a criminal could get to a church without being captured, he or she could stay there without being arrested. These people were free to leave the church if they admitted that they were guilty and agreed to leave the country.

SOURCE D

Sanctuary continued throughout the Middle Ages. It did not always work out according to the rules.

'A wicked man from Brittany murdered a widow in her bed outside Aldgate in the suburbs of London. He carried away all the money she had and took sanctuary in the holy church of St George in Southwark. He finally agreed to leave the church in return for permission to leave the country. As he left, he passed near the place where he had committed murder. There the women of the area came out to meet him with stones and dung and they stoned him to death.'

The Brut Chronicle, fifteenth century

The world of the manor courts

Minor crimes were dealt with in local manor courts. The judge was usually one of the officials of the local lord. The punishments were usually fines, which were paid to the lord. These manor courts also dealt with the organisation of farming in the area.

SOURCE E

'Beton, the maid of Richard Walker, was guilty of assault on Jane, wife of Thomas Merriman. She hit her so hard that blood was shed. She is fined 3s. 4d. [17p]'

Manor Court Records of Durham Priory, fourteenth century

---

1 What is the difference between a royal court and a manor court?

2 Thomas the village priest discovers a silver cross has been stolen from the church. Godfrey is accused of the crime, but he denies it.
Explain what would have happened to Godfrey under each of the following circumstances:
a if the crime happened in 1100
b if the crime happened in 1200
c if Godfrey were a priest
d if Godfrey sought sanctuary in the church.

3 Why do you think people in the Middle Ages treated suspected criminals in different ways?

4 What might happen to Godfrey if he had committed the crime today?

5 Do you think the modern system of law and order is fairer than the medieval system?

16

Yorkshire 1219

In 1219 the royal judges visited Yorkshire. The following cases are a small selection of the sort of case that a royal judge had to deal with.

What can we learn from these cases about medieval law and order?

CASE 1

'Robert de Engelby killed William of Hilton and fled to the local church for sanctuary. He admitted that he was guilty and was allowed to leave the country.'

CASE 2

'Jordan the Tall accuses Simon of Duffield of wickedly coming by night to the house of Hawisa, his niece, with his son, William, and two daughters. Having broken into the house, Simon strangled Hawisa with a cord. Jordan saw them going in and raised the alarm. Simon says he is not guilty. It is ordered that a duel should take place between Simon and Jordan. Simon loses the duel and is hanged.'

CASE 3

'William the miller of Leathley killed Henry of Leathley and Theobald of Leathley. He ran away but was captured and beheaded on the spot. The court took his goods, which were worth 1 mark [67p].'

CASE 4

'John of Thornton goes about the country with a gang of fifteen horsemen and he has used Richmond Castle as a base. He came to Richmond about Christmas time with some expensive cloth and dressed his men as if he was a baron. Everywhere they go they rob.'

CASE 5

'The jury of the town of Doncaster say that William Talbot, Robert Burgate and their gang have been to Doncaster. They attacked the town and killed Robert of Aylesham and his son, Thomas, and burned down eight houses and did £500 worth of damage. Hugh Lupus says that he was wounded in the stomach with a lance and that he almost had his hand cut off.'

SOURCE A

A violent robbery. How common a sight was this in thirteenth-century Yorkshire?

CASE 6

'Simon le Vacher was arrested for burning down the houses of Henry of Silton and put in prison in York. He escaped from prison and went to a church for sanctuary. He was allowed to leave the country.'

CASE 7

'Thomas Waghepol was killed in Crofton Field. Adam the Shepherd found him. They say that strangers killed him and they do not know who they were, but they stole twenty-four pigs, each worth 12d. [5p]'

CASE 8

'Hugh Sturdy wounded Henry the Foolish so that he died and Hugh ran away. Let him be outlawed. The court could not take his goods as he had none.'

CASE 9

'John of Cleaving was outlawed some time ago for killing his wife's brother. One day he returned to the village and stayed at the house of Rannulf of Cleaving. For this Rannulf should be arrested. It is said that the outlaw held a drinking session and the following should be arrested for being present at this ale-drinking: Rannulf, Ralf Takell, Godfrey and his brothers Richard and Thomas, Warin, Martin, Serlo and Walter Swart. The whole village of Cleaving will be fined because they did not capture the outlaw.'

CASE 10

'Wicked people came by night to the house of William le Vacher of Raisdale, burnt his house and killed him. Simon the Monk and nine others are suspected. They have all run away and are outlawed. The people of the village say that Simon was a doctor and often visited a neighbour's house to cure the neighbour's wife, who was sick. Simon and the lady became lovers. Simon used William le Vacher as a messenger to the lady. One day William heard Simon and his gang say they were going to kill the neighbour. William tried to warn him, so Simon went to William's house and killed him.'

Many of the Yorkshire criminals were declared to be outlaws. If they were caught they could be executed without a trial.

SOURCE B

Criminals were sometimes beheaded on the spot when captured. This picture comes from a fourteenth-century manuscript. Which case describes such an incident?

Imagine that you were one of the royal judges who visited Yorkshire. The government in London is eager to know what is happening in the north, and has asked you and the other judges to produce a report on law and order in Yorkshire.

a Work in a small group. Each of you is a judge. Discuss the cases you have tried in Yorkshire, and explain why you have given these punishments.

b Working individually, write your own report on the crimes and punishments.

17

The power of the Church

> *Thousands of modern British villages are built on the site of a medieval village. In many of them, only one medieval building has survived to the present day – the church. It is no coincidence that the churches have remained, while most medieval houses have been destroyed.*
>
> **Why was the Church so important in the Middle Ages?**

SOURCE A
An angel locking the door to hell. The Church said that people who broke its rules would stay in a place like this for ever. This picture was painted in the twelfth century.

Look at these two statements:
a 'The Church was important because it frightened people.'
b 'The Church was important because it helped people.'
Find evidence in the unit to support each statement. The statements give two different reasons. Does that mean that one of them must be untrue?

Stone among timber

Churches were built of the best stone, while ordinary houses were usually made of wood and thatch. This fact shows us how important the church was in a medieval village. In this unit you will be able to find out why the Church played a big part in the lives of people in the Middle Ages.

Heaven or hell?

Between 1066 and 1500 nearly everyone who lived in Britain was a Christian. They all belonged to the Catholic Church. They believed that it was through the work of the priests that they could come to know God and make sure of a place in heaven after death. The priests taught people that if they broke too many of the rules laid down by the Church, they would suffer for ever in the horrible world of hell.

SOURCE B

The Church taught everyone that after death there would be a Day of Judgement when everyone would stand before God to see if they would go to heaven or to hell.

'God will sit as a stern judge above all the people. Sinners will suffer great misery as the horrible pit of hell opens up. Large numbers of devils will appear to drag them to the torture and burning of hell.'

Anselm, Archbishop of Canterbury, late eleventh century

The importance of relics

People believed that they were more likely to get into heaven if they prayed to the saints. These were holy men and women who were already in heaven. A piece from the body of a dead saint was known as a 'relic'. Relics were thought to have a special power that could help people with their prayers. Most churches had relics, and big abbeys and cathedrals had the relics of very famous saints. People would travel many miles to visit a church containing such a relic, and after praying they would give money to the priests who looked after the church.

SOURCE C

There was great rivalry between different churches over relics. Leading bishops and abbots always wanted to get the best relics for their own church.

'When Bishop Hugh was at the famous monastery of Fécamp, he got two small pieces of the arm of St Mary Magdalen by biting them from the bone. When the abbot and monks saw what their visitor was doing, they got very cross. They shouted out, "How terrible. He has stuck his teeth into the bone and gnawed at it, as if he was a dog." '

The Life of St Hugh, Bishop of Lincoln, late twelfth century

The surest way to heaven

It was widely believed that the best way of making sure of getting into heaven after death was by becoming a monk or a nun. Both monks and nuns were supposed to follow a strict rule involving long hours of prayer and work.

In the early Middle Ages rich people gave lots of their land and their money to the Church, and especially to the monasteries and nunneries. In return, they expected the priests, monks and nuns to say special prayers for them, to help them get to heaven. As a result, the Church became very wealthy. Many ordinary country people had a bishop or a monastery as their landlord.

SOURCE D

The Church built huge barns to hold all the crops that it received from the people. Many of these barns can still be seen today. This barn is at Harmondsworth in Middlesex.

Special treatment

The Church had a number of important privileges. All people were expected to give one-tenth of their income or crops as a tax to the Church; these payments were called 'tithes'. There were countless arguments in the countryside between villagers and priests about the payment of tithes.

Priests could not be tried in ordinary courts if they broke the law. Instead they were dealt with by special Church courts, which usually imposed lighter penalties.

SOURCE E

'William de Word was arrested for killing William de Lavington. He pleads that he is a clergyman. In a fight outside Salisbury Cathedral at curfew, William de Word struck the other William with a knife in his right arm under the elbow; he died of his wound in less than a fortnight. The court ordered that he should be handed over to the bishop to be tried in the Church court.'

Salisbury Gaol Records, 1293

Reading, writing and ruling

Clergymen were among the best-educated people in the Middle Ages. In many villages the local priest would be important as the only person who could read and write. At a higher level, priests and bishops often worked as government civil servants or ministers because they were so well educated.

A source of help

There were not many schools or hospitals in the Middle Ages. The few that did exist were usually run by the Church. Priests also helped the very poorest people by encouraging the better-off to give 'alms' or charity. Priests themselves were expected to give back some of the money they got from tithes as charity for the poor. Some monasteries had a good reputation for looking after local poor people.

SOURCE F

'During the terrible famine of 1197, our monastery, although it was new and did not have much money, gave help to many. On a single day, 1,500 poor people gathered at the monastery gates and were given help. On some days the abbot had a whole ox stewed and he gave out a ration with bread to every poor person.'

Cesarius of Heisterbach, *Dialogue of Miracles*, early thirteenth century

The Church and its enemies

Today many people in Britain do not believe in Christianity. In medieval times, nearly everyone did. The Christian Church was an important part of people's lives. But was everyone a firm believer in the Church's teaching?

There do seem to have been some people who were so badly educated that they knew very little about Christianity.

SOURCE G

This is taken from a sermon preached by an English priest.

'A traveller once stopped and asked a shepherd if he knew the Father, the Son and the Holy Ghost. The shepherd replied, "I know the Father and the Son for I look after their sheep, but I haven't heard of the other fellow. No one of that name lives in our village." '

The Sermons of Bromyard, late fourteenth century

Among wealthy people, there were a few who were not frightened of hell and wanted to have a good time in this world.

SOURCE H

This extract is from a popular medieval story. A man called Aucassin has just been told that he might go to hell if he keeps on seeing his girl-friend, Nicolette. This is how Aucassin replies.

'Why should I want to go to heaven? I would not wish to go there unless I can have Nicolette, because I love her so much. I want nothing to do with the sort of people who will go to heaven, doddering old priests and fools who grovel in church all day and night. I'd rather be in hell with those handsome knights killed in battle and other noble men, with those lovely noble ladies who have lots of lovers.'

Aucassin and Nicolette, written in France about 1200

Heretics

Sometimes people came up with new ideas that the Church did not like. The Church called these people heretics. Heretics were still Christians, but they did not agree with what the Catholic Church taught.

There seem to have been very few heretics in Britain before the fourteenth century, but occasionally heretics from the rest of Europe tried to find recruits in Britain.

SOURCE I

A group of German Cathars (heretics) was arrested at Oxford in the late twelfth century.

'The king commanded that they should be branded upon the forehead, flogged and driven out of Oxford. Their clothes were cut to their waists so that they could be beaten, then they were thrown out of the city. Nobody helped them and they died a miserable death.'

William of Newburgh, *History of England,* about 1200

The rebellion of the Lollards

The only important group of British heretics were the Lollards in the fourteenth and fifteenth centuries. They were followers of a writer called John Wyclif, who died in 1384. The Lollards believed that the Bible, which was only available in Latin, should be produced in English so that more people could read it for themselves. They did not like the complex ceremonies performed in Latin by the priests; they wanted simpler church services. They also said that the Church had too much land and money.

The English government passed a law in 1401 which said that 'if anyone is found guilty of preaching Lollard ideas, the mayor or sheriff should have them burnt in a public place'. Surviving Lollards were forced to keep their beliefs a secret from the government.

---

1 Look at Source I. Was the king pleased that the Cathars had visited Britain?

2 Explain in your own words why the Lollards did not like the Catholic Church.

3 What reasons can you think of to explain why the Cathars and Lollards were so badly treated? Why do you think the Church reacted so strongly to heretics?

The wider world of Christendom

Until the middle of the twentieth century, many people in Britain saw themselves as part of a worldwide British Empire. Today we see ourselves more and more as part of the European Community. In the Middle Ages people talked about belonging to Christendom – the lands where Christianity was the main religion. For British people, the heartland of Christendom was that part of Western Europe where the Roman Catholic Church was followed (the Western Church). The Pope in Rome led the Church and Latin was used as the language of the Church.

Beyond Christendom

Parts of Eastern Europe, such as Greece and Russia, were Christian, but not Roman Catholic. They belonged to the Orthodox Church (Eastern Church) which had its headquarters in Constantinople (modern Istanbul).

On the edges of Christendom, from Spain to modern Turkey, were Islamic countries. Both Christendom and Islam wanted to control Jerusalem because it was a very holy place in the two religions. This conflict led to the wars over Jerusalem that we call the Crusades. There were seven Crusades between 1099 and 1248.

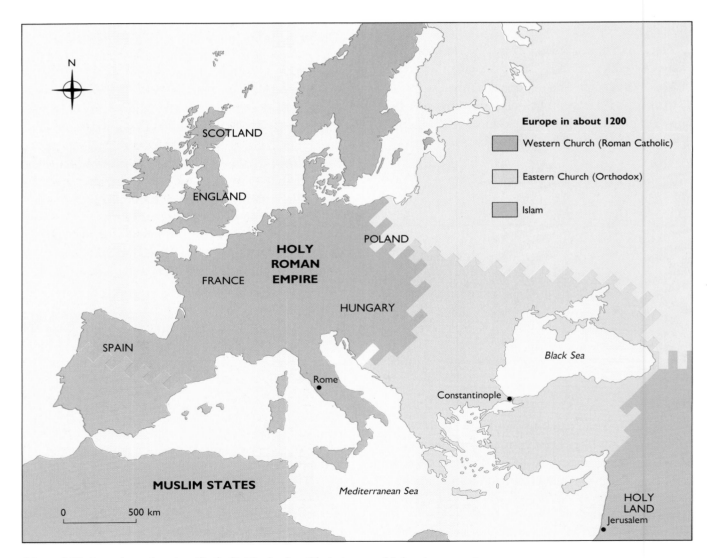

Map of Christendom showing Catholic/Orthodox Christian, and Islamic countries.

Monks and nuns

> *Some men and women gave up their whole lives to the Church. They left behind the ordinary world, and joined a monastery or nunnery.*
>
> *What was life like for a monk or nun in medieval times?*

The rule of Saint Benedict

In 1066 all monks and nuns in Britain were Benedictine. This meant that they were supposed to follow the strict rule laid down by St Benedict, an Italian monk of the sixth century. The rule said that monks should spend nearly all of their time praying or working. Monks and nuns were supposed to live very simply: they were not allowed to have any possessions of their own; they were supposed to have only two simple meals a day, and were not allowed meat unless they were ill; and they were not allowed to get married. The head of each monastery or nunnery was called the abbot or abbess, and each monk or nun had to obey them completely.

Monks and nuns made three strict promises or vows. These vows were to help them to lead holy lives.

Look at these descriptions of life in different Benedictine monasteries.

SOURCE A

Orderic Vitalis was an English monk who spent most of his life in a French monastery.

'Consider how hard life is in a monastery. We are the soldiers of Christ fighting bravely against the devil. It is impossible to describe all the prayers, hymns and masses we say each day. Our clothes are plain, we have little food and drink and we cannot do as we please.'

Orderic Vitalis, *Ecclesiastical History*, early twelfth century

SOURCE B

A monk of St Albans Abbey wrote the following description of his abbot, William, shortly after the abbot's death.

'When he came back from a journey, he used to invite all the poor people from outside the monastery gates and he arranged for them to be fed. He went to all the services, even on weekdays, and he used to set an enthusiastic example with his singing. He only ate his meals at the set time. He studied holy books and was a wise teacher.'

Matthew Paris, written in about 1235

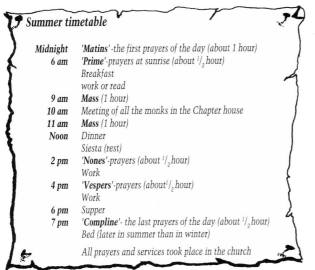

Summer timetable

Midnight	'Matins' -the first prayers of the day (about 1 hour)
6 am	'Prime' -prayers at sunrise (about $\frac{1}{2}$ hour)
	Breakfast
	work or read
9 am	**Mass** (1 hour)
10 am	Meeting of all the monks in the Chapter house
11 am	**Mass** (1 hour)
Noon	Dinner
	Siesta (rest)
2 pm	'Nones' -prayers (about $\frac{1}{2}$ hour)
	Work
4 pm	'Vespers' -prayers (about $\frac{1}{2}$ hour)
	Work
6 pm	Supper
7 pm	'**Compline**'- the last prayers of the day (about $\frac{1}{2}$ hour)
	Bed (later in summer than in winter)
	All prayers and services took place in the church

Many monks and nuns followed a timetable like this. How many times a day did they go to church?

SOURCE C

The monastery of Bury St Edmunds was one of the richest Benedictine houses.

'When Samson became abbot, he spent a day of celebration with over a thousand dinner guests rejoicing greatly. As abbot he had several parks made for the abbey. He stocked them with wild animals and kept a huntsman and hounds. If an important guest was visiting, the abbot and his monks would sit in a clearing and watch the hunt.'

Jocelin of Brakelond, *Chronicle*, early thirteenth century

A new order arrives in Britain

A new group of monks emerged in the early twelfth century. They were called Cistercians after a place in France, Cîteaux, where they built their first monastery. The first Cistercians, led by a French abbot, Bernard of Clairvaux, felt that the Benedictines were too soft. They wanted to get back to the strict spirit of St Benedict's original rule. The Cistercians built new monasteries in remote places where few people lived, such as Rievaulx and Fountains in Yorkshire. As well as spending many hours each day in church, the Cistercians also did hard physical work as farmers in the local area.

SOURCE D

William of Malmesbury was a Benedictine monk. He wrote a description of the lifestyle of the rival Cistercian monks.

'Many of their rules are strict. They sleep with their clothes on. No one is allowed to miss prayers unless they are ill. From September to Easter they only have one meal a day, except on Sunday. They never go outside the monastery except to work, and they do not speak except to the abbot.'

William of Malmesbury, writing in about 1140

SOURCE E

Not everyone liked the new monks. This description was written by a civil servant.

'The Cistercians work so hard that they have become very rich, but they are mean and do not like to spend their wealth. They are happy to borrow farming equipment from others, but they will not lend anyone their ploughs. Their rule does not allow them to work as parish priests, so when they are given new lands they destroy any villages there and throw out the people who live there.'

Walter Map, *Courtiers' Trifles*, late twelfth century

● Do the Sources D and E agree on the Cistercians?

SOURCE F

By the end of the Middle Ages, some monks and nuns lived comfortable lives. This indoor toilet is at Mount Grace Priory. It would be many centuries before ordinary people had indoor toilets.

The friars come preaching

In the thirteenth century, a hundred years after the Cistercians had appeared, a very different type of religious order developed, known as the friars. The first friars were followers of an Italian, Francis of Assisi. Unlike the monks, the friars did not live in abbeys, but travelled about preaching, working and begging. The first friars thought that monasteries had grown too rich, and they tried to keep themselves completely poor.

By the late Middle Ages, members of the religious orders had become less popular than in earlier centuries. At the end of the fourteenth century the poet Geoffrey Chaucer wrote his *Canterbury Tales*. He included descriptions of a typical nun and monk.

SOURCE G

By the late Middle Ages, many people had a low opinion of monks and nuns. What is this monk doing? This picture comes from a thirteenth-century manuscript.

SOURCE H

The Nun
'She was called Madam Eglentine and she sang well in church. She had some small dogs as pets, and she fed them roast meat, milk and expensive bread. She cried if one of the dogs got hurt. She took pride in her appearance and wore ornaments of coral and gold.'

The Monk
'He was a powerful man that loved riding and hunting, and he had many fine horses in the stables. He cared little for the old strict rules. He said that he would not waste his time studying books in the cloisters or working with his hands. He had some greyhounds for hunting hare that were as fast as birds. His sleeves were trimmed with grey fur. He loved to eat roast swan.'

Geoffrey Chaucer, *Canterbury Tales*, fourteenth century

● What can we learn from Chaucer about how these people lived?

---

1 A television producer is making a programme on the lives of monks and nuns in the Middle Ages. She wants to investigate whether they led a simple, holy life, or whether they led lives of selfish pleasure. She gets in touch with two historians.

Work as a pair. One of you is a historian on the side of the monks and nuns, the other thinks they were selfish. Using the sources in the unit produce statements of:
a evidence that monks and nuns led simple, holy lives

b evidence that monks and nuns were only interested in pleasure. You will need to explain why the evidence you have chosen can be trusted.

2 Stay in the same pair. Now you are a team of scriptwriters employed by the producer. She gives you the information from the two historians but says she wants a TV script that is balanced and shows that the monks and nuns were a mixture of good and bad. Write the script and produce examples of the sources you will use in the programme.

19

Looking after the sick

> Medieval doctors used ideas that Greek and Roman doctors had written down many hundreds of years earlier. From these ancient writings they got the idea that the body contained four liquids or humours. If the humours got out of balance, the patient would become ill.
>
> How did medieval medicine differ from modern medicine?

Well-paid doctors

A variety of men and women looked after the sick in medieval times. Most of them expected to be paid for their work. The most expensive were doctors, and usually only the rich could afford to use them.

SOURCE A

'Doctors have two favourite sayings, "Do not work where there is no money" and "Get your fee while the patient is in pain". Truly, they think it is beneath them to help the poor if they cannot pay them.'

John of Salisbury, about 1150

SOURCE B

Medieval doctors thought you could tell the cause of sickness by studying the colour of patients' urine.

SOURCE C

Abbot John of St Albans was a doctor as well as a monk. Matthew Paris describes how, when he was dying, he examined his own urine.

'The next day he looked carefully at his urine to see what would happen to him, for he was a good doctor and one of the best judges of urine. However, his eyesight had become poor so that he could not see the secret signs of death that he was looking for. So he asked another monk, Master William the Doctor, to inspect the urine. The abbot was told that he had three days left to live.'

Matthew Paris, thirteenth century

Horoscopes and bleeding patients

Doctors also believed in astrology. They thought that the stars and planets had an impact on how well or ill people felt. In the fourteenth century, Chaucer explained how a doctor worked out his patient's horoscope before deciding on the treatment. A remedy might involve draining some blood from the patient, or getting a potion of drugs from the drug-sellers or apothecaries. There were some women doctors in the thirteenth century, but when the universities took control of the training of doctors, they would not let women have a licence.

Painful surgery

Doctors themselves rarely ran the risk of getting dirty by operating on their patients or cutting them to draw off their blood. These jobs were left to surgeons, who were less well paid and often combined surgery with the job of being a barber. Operations could only be simple and were very painful because they had no proper pain-killers.

> ### SOURCE D
> This is an extract from a book of instructions for surgeons.
>
> 'Surgeons should try to look sober and not drunk. They should not look too closely at the lady of the house, and they should not kiss her. They should wear plain clothes and not dress up like a minstrel. They should try to cheer up their patients by telling them to be brave when they are in great pain. It is useful if surgeons can tell good jokes to make their patients laugh.'
>
> John of Arderne, about 1370

SOURCE E
A surgeon at work. How does this compare with modern operating practice?

Other sources of help

People who could not afford to go to doctors or surgeons would seek much cheaper medical help. Much of this was provided by women. There were midwives to help with childbirth. Many villages would have a 'wise woman' able to give the sick traditional mixtures of herbs for different illnesses.

Dealing with mental illness

Men and women with a physical disability or mental illness often have a difficult life today. Such people faced much greater hardship in the Middle Ages. Those with mental illness got no help and were often badly treated. A lawbook of the early twelfth century mentions that 'madmen' were put on show with wild animals at country fairs.

> ### SOURCE F
> This is how a monk of St Albans was treated when he became mentally ill.
>
> 'The abbot was worried to hear of Alexander's madness. He summoned him to a meeting of the monks, where he had him flogged until the blood flowed freely. Even after this Alexander did not behave himself, so the abbot had him chained and kept in solitary confinement until he died.'
>
> Matthew Paris, thirteenth century

● Copy this table, comparing modern and medieval medicine. Fill in the information about medieval medicine.

Modern	Medieval
Doctors Most doctors in Britain work for the National Health Service.	
Surgeons Some doctors do more training and work as surgeons. They are very skilful and highly paid.	
Other health workers (e.g. nurses, midwives, chemists, physiotherapists)	
Mental illness The mentally ill are treated by doctors.	

20

The Black Death

The Black Death was one of the greatest human disasters in European history. The epidemic spread through England and Wales in 1348 and 1349. By 1350 it had reached Scotland. We do not have exact figures, but most historians think that about a third of the population of Britain was killed by the Black Death.

How did people at the time explain the disease?

SOURCE A

A monk collapses from the plague while Church leaders beg God to stop the disease. From a fifteenth-century manuscript.

Fleas, rats and microbes

Nowadays we call the disease the bubonic plague. Modern science has shown that the cause is a tiny micro-organism, so small that it can only be seen under a microscope. This minute germ was carried by fleas, which themselves lived on black rats. As the rats moved across Europe, they took the Black Death with them.

SOURCE B

One of the best descriptions of the terrible impact of the plague was written by the Italian poet, Boccaccio, who was in Florence at the time of the Black Death.

'In both men and women the disease showed itself by the appearance of a round swelling in the groin or the armpits. Some of these swellings were the size of an apple or an egg. The swellings spread across the body and black or red spots then appeared. It spread from sick people to the healthy. People caught it if they visited the sick or if they just touched the clothes of the sick.'

Boccaccio, *The Decameron*, fourteenth century

SOURCE C

An unknown writer wrote this description of how he thought the Black Death had started in the Far East.

'The disease was carried in the air by a foul blast of wind that came from the South and grew more poisonous day by day.'

Anonymous Flemish priest, fourteenth century

SOURCE D

The Black Death arrived in Dorset in August 1348 and then slowly spread across the whole of Britain.

'Many people died in Dorset and then it spread violently throughout Devon and Somerset as far as Bristol. The people of Gloucester would not let those of Bristol come to Gloucestershire, for they believed that their breath was infected. Despite this, it eventually reached Gloucester.'

Geoffrey le Baker, fourteenth century

SOURCE E
Burying victims of the plague at Tournai in 1349. A Flemish picture painted in 1352.

---

1 Using information from the sources, work out how many different explanations for the Black Death (and its spreading) people had at the time.

2 Can you think of any reasons why medieval people came up with so many different explanations?

3 How useful are the sources for finding out about medicine in the Middle Ages?

A chronicle of

1066–1150 The Normans build motte and bailey castles across Britain

There were hardly any castles in Britain before 1066. The Normans built simple motte and bailey castles of earth and timber wherever they went. From the start, they built a few very important castles out of stone, such as the Tower of London.

1066–1500 Enormous abbeys and cathedrals are built

The greatest buildings of the Middle Ages were the cathedrals. They show how rich and important the Church was at the time. The style of building changed as years went by. You can work out the date of a building by the shape of its windows and arches.

1280–1300 Edward I establishes a line of castles across north Wales

Castles developed a lot from the basic motte and bailey design. The finest castles were the work of Edward I. He built a series of magnificent stone castles across north Wales in order to stop the Welsh from rebelling.

1200–1300 Universities are set up at Oxford and Cambridge

At the time of the Conquest there was little study and high-level teaching except in abbeys. This changed in the thirteenth century when Oxford and Cambridge universities were founded. They trained people to do important jobs as lawyers and government officials.

medieval culture

There were no permanent theatres in the Middle Ages, although there were wandering musicians, jugglers and acrobats. In the late fourteenth century, workers in towns like York and Wakefield started putting on religious drama, which they called 'miracle plays'.

1350–1500 Craft guilds in towns start to put on 'miracle plays'

The Normans spoke French, and for many centuries English was not a respectable language. Writers nearly always used French or Latin. This changed in the fourteenth century when English began to take over from French. A pioneer of the use of English was the great poet, Chaucer, who wrote the *Canterbury Tales*.

1370–1400 Chaucer writes his fine poetry in English

In 1066 most people could not read and write. Only priests and monks used books and wrote letters. At the end of the Middle Ages, country folk were still unable to write, but wealthier men and women were much better educated. Many personal letters have survived, such as those of the rich Norfolk woman, Margaret Paston.

1450–80 Margaret Paston writes her letters

When William Caxton brought printing from Germany to London in 1477, it was the beginning of a new age. Before that every single book had been handwritten and as a result books were very scarce. Many of the handwritten books had been produced in abbeys.

1477 William Caxton produces the first printed books in Britain

21

Building the castles and cathedrals

Almost everywhere you go in Britain it is possible to see castles and cathedrals built during the Middle Ages. They were constructed by huge armies of stonemasons and carpenters.

What was life like for the people who built the castles and cathedrals?

SOURCE A
Builders and masons at work. From a thirteenth-century manuscript. Can you work out what each man is doing?

Who was in charge?

The builders were not a single group. At the top was the master mason who was responsible for designing as well as building. The master masons were important men and they were well paid. The records of Vale Royal Abbey in Cheshire show that in 1278 the master mason was being paid more than fifteen times the wages of a labourer. We know many of their names from building accounts. One of the greatest of master masons was James of St George, who was in charge of the castles built for Edward I in Wales. The king had him brought all the way from Savoy in southern France to work for him.

Forced labour

The government had the power to 'conscript' building workers; that is, force them to leave home and come and work on a particular building. Edward I used this power when he was building his castles in north Wales in the late thirteenth century.

Building work began at dawn. Workers would usually have half an hour off for breakfast. They had a longer break for lunch, and were sometimes allowed a short sleep before starting the afternoon shift. Work continued in the evening until about 7 o'clock. Sunday was usually a day off, and work stopped at lunchtime on Saturdays.

Managing a large force of building workers could be difficult.

SOURCE E

Durham Cathedral: a massive Norman cathedral.

SOURCE F

The nave of Durham Cathedral with its huge Norman pillars.

◄ **SOURCE D**

Conway Castle in north Wales. What problems did Master James of St George have when building this castle?

1 Why were master masons important people on medieval building sites?

2 What different types of worker would you find helping to build castles and cathedrals?

3 What can we learn from Sources B and C about the problems of being a master mason?

4 How do the buildings themselves help you to understand better the lives of the builders?

5 'Life was hard for the builders of the castles and cathedrals.' Would you agree with this?

22

The English language

The English language changed a lot during the Middle Ages. If you went back in time to 1066, you would find it very difficult to understand what ordinary people in towns and villages were saying. The language did not begin to sound like modern English until about 1500.

Where does modern English come from?

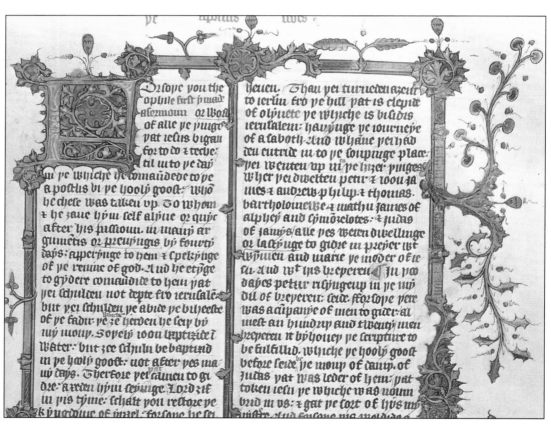

SOURCE A

A late medieval manuscript showing writing in English. Can you identify any words?

Back to Anglo-Saxon roots

A lot of everyday English words come from Anglo-Saxon, the language used in England in 1066.

Look at the two columns of words on the next page. On the left-hand side are some common English words that we use today, and on the right-hand side are the Anglo-Saxon (Old English) words that they come from.

Although the Old English looks like a foreign language, it is not hard to see how it has changed over the centuries to become modern English.

Modern English	Anglo-Saxon (Old English)
day	daeg
noon	non
week	wice
month	mōnath
year	geār
mother	modor
go	gan
drink	drincan

A mixture of tongues

Old English was not the only language spoken in medieval Britain. Many Welsh and Scottish people spoke Celtic languages.

The year 1066 was an important turning-point in the development of the English language. The Normans who came to England with William the Conqueror in 1066 spoke French. French now became the language of the Court, the government and the nobles. For three centuries after the Conquest, many of the books written in England were in French, even though ordinary people carried on speaking Old English.

● Explain in your own words how the English language changed 1066–1500.

Latin was the language of the Catholic Church. All church services were conducted in Latin, and the Bible was written in Latin. Latin was also the language of international communication – kings, queens, princes, bishops and nobles all over Europe could speak Latin.

● What language is used today for international communication?

In time, the English language borrowed words from French and Latin. As a result, our modern English language has a very rich and varied mixture of different words from different countries.

Look at the following tables of words from Old English, Old French and Latin.

Modern English	Old English	Modern English	Old French	Latin
ox	oxa	beef	boeuf	bos
calf	cealf	veal	veēl	
sheep	sceap	mutton	mouton	
pig	picga	pork	porc	porcus

● What is the difference between the meaning of the words in the two modern English lists? Why do you think one list comes from the Old English and one list comes from Old French? (Remember that the Normans who came over with William were nobles, not farmers.)

The triumph of English

In the fourteenth century, there was a growing feeling that people should use English if they had something important to write or say. Members of Parliament started conducting their meetings in English, rather than French. For the first time since the Conquest of 1066, serious writers wrote in English. Some people started asking for the Bible to be written in English, so that more people could read it. The next unit discusses two important writers, Geoffrey Chaucer and Margaret Paston.

23

Two English writers

In the early Middle Ages few people, other than priests, monks and nuns, could read and write, and almost all books were written in Latin or French. This changed after 1350. More and more men and women outside the Church learned how to write. Increasingly, it became respectable to write in English.

What examples of writing in English do we have from the Middle Ages?

In this unit you can see examples of medieval writing in English. The first extracts are by the great English poet, Geoffrey Chaucer, who wrote the *Canterbury Tales* in the late fourteenth century. The second section is taken from the letters of a rich Norfolk woman called Margaret Paston, who wrote in the mid-fifteenth century.

What can we learn from their writings about how men and women got on in the Middle Ages?

Geoffrey Chaucer

The *Canterbury Tales* are about a number of people who are going to Canterbury on a pilgrimage. As they travel, they tell different stories to pass the time.

SOURCE A

Geoffrey Chaucer. This picture comes from a fifteenth-century manuscript.

SOURCE B

One of the most interesting pilgrims is known as the Wife of Bath.

'Since I was twelve, I have been married five times at the church-door. Each husband has done as I told him, and each was happy to bring me presents from the fair. Often I spoke fiercely to them, so that they were relieved when I was pleasant.'

Chaucer, *The Wife of Bath's Prologue*

SOURCE C

The last part of the *Canterbury Tales* is a sermon by the parson, who was one of the pilgrims. His thoughts are probably typical of many priests in the late Middle Ages.

'A woman should do as she is told by her husband. As a wife, she should not be a witness in court without her husband's permission. Women should aim to please their husbands, but not by wearing fancy clothes. A wife should try to look sensible and not laugh too much and gossip.'

Chaucer, *The Parson's Tale*

Margaret Paston

Margaret Paston was a member of a wealthy land-owning family in fifteenth-century Norfolk. Her husband, John, was away in London on business for much of the time. In his absence Margaret ran the large Norfolk farms that they owned.

Most rich people like Margaret and John Paston had 'arranged' marriages. This meant that they did not choose to marry each other freely – their parents decided that they should get married and arranged the wedding. Parents usually tried to get a husband or wife for their child who was as rich as possible.

SOURCE E
A fifteenth-century picture of a wealthy woman writing.

SOURCE D

Although they had an arranged marriage, Margaret seems to have loved John very much. She wrote this letter when she heard that he had been ill.

'In truth, I have never had such a sad time as I had when I knew of your sickness until the time when I knew of your getting better. I wish you were at home so that your sore might be well looked after.'

Paston, *Letters*

SOURCE F

After her daughter got married to poor Richard Calle without permission, Margaret wrote this letter to one of her sons. She told him not to get too upset about the fact that they would not be seeing Margery again because of her disgrace.

'I beg and demand that you take it not too badly for I know well how you feel. You should remember, as I do, that in her we have lost a worthless person. Even if Calle died this very hour, she should not be close to my heart as she once was.'

Paston, *Letters*

When her own children were older, Margaret spent much of her time trying to arrange their marriages. With one of them she failed. Her daughter, Margery, fell in love with one of their servants, Richard Calle. Marrying someone much poorer than yourself was thought a disgrace and Margaret tried very hard to stop their wedding. Despite this, Margery married Richard. Margaret told her daughter that she never wanted to see her again and she was not allowed inside Margaret's house.

Fifteenth-century Norfolk was a very violent place. Some powerful men used force to take farms, houses and castles from their neighbours. Margaret seems to have been very tough in dealing with these bandits. According to one letter she was once in a manor house with twelve servants when hundreds of armed men appeared; she refused to give in and had to be dragged out of the building.

Imagine that you are a journalist working for a weekly magazine. Your editor has told you to do an article on marriage in the Middle Ages entitled 'Did medieval husbands and wives get on well together?'

You only have a few days to write the article so you decide to concentrate on the examples of marriage shown in the writings of Chaucer and Margaret Paston. Using the evidence from this unit, write the article and try to answer the question in the article title.

24

A medieval legacy

Much has changed since 1500, but the world of the Middle Ages still has an impact on the way we live today. At first glance London, with its cars and high-rise offices and flats, is a very modern place. However, if we take a closer look, there are countless links between the present and medieval times.

Street names
The names of some streets, such as Milk Street and Bread Street, can tell us a lot about medieval London's trade areas. Food markets of today, such as Smithfield, the great meat market, and Billingsgate, a huge fish market, also survive from medieval times.

The Tower of London
The mighty White Tower was built by William the Conqueror. The Tower of London was always a fortress and an armoury. In the last 900 years it has also been used as a top prison, a place of execution and a safe place to keep the priceless Crown jewels.

Westminster Hall
The Lords and Commons used to meet here for Parliaments. The hall was built of stone in the late eleventh century, but the roof was added nearly 300 years later. Its oak 'hammerbeam' roof is a masterpiece of medieval carpentry.

Westminster Abbey
This medieval abbey has been the scene of nearly every royal coronation since 1066. William the Conqueror was crowned in Westminster Abbey on Christmas Day, 1066, and the present queen was crowned here in 1953.

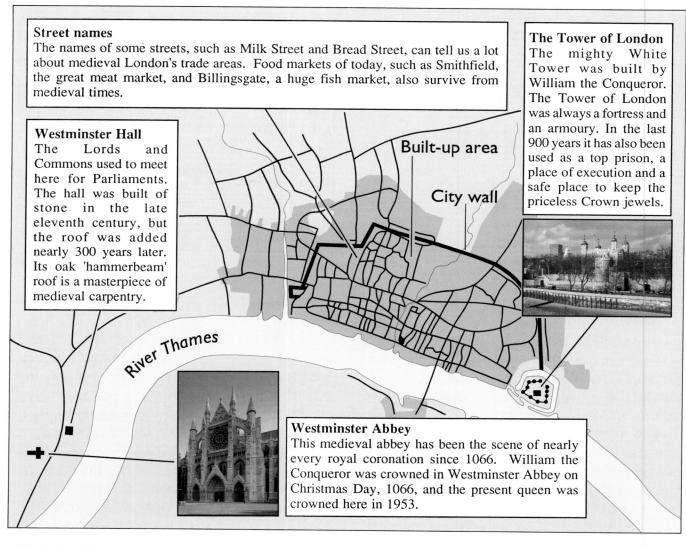

Built-up area

City wall

River Thames

The sights of modern London – their roots lie deep in the Middle Ages.

London: a modern city?

Tourists who come to London usually visit its old buildings. Two of the most popular tourist attractions are Westminster Abbey and the Tower of London, both of which were built in the Middle Ages. Westminster Abbey was founded by Edward the Confessor before 1066, and re-built in the thirteenth century by Henry III. It was a royal church in the Middle Ages, and it continues to be so today as the scene of many royal weddings and funerals.

The Tower of London was begun by William the Conqueror immediately after his victory at Hastings. Although it has been changed over the years, you can still see the White Tower that William built in the eleventh century. Other abbeys and castles can be seen in every part of Britain. Some are in ruins, others are still used today, many centuries after their foundation.

Law and order

You have probably seen the outside of the Old Bailey on television. It is one of the most important courts in Britain, and many serious trials have been held there. The modern system of courts can be traced back to the Middle Ages. For example, the idea of using a jury of ordinary people to decide if someone is guilty was developed in the twelfth century.

The origins of Parliament

The Houses of Parliament are famous throughout the world. Most of the buildings you see today are not very old, but Parliament has met on this site since the Middle Ages. Parliament is very different now from medieval times, but some elements remain from the first Parliaments of the thirteenth and fourteenth centuries. For example, the division of Parliament into the House of Lords and the House of Commons goes right back to the Middle Ages.

Queen and country

Visitors to modern London often hope to see the queen, or other members of the royal family. Popular newspapers are full of 'royal' stories. There is a direct link between the modern royal family and the kings and queens of the Middle Ages. The modern royal family does not have much power but still plays an important part in official ceremonies.

Ancient highways

All the ordinary buildings of medieval London are long gone. They have either been demolished or accidentally burned down. However, the layout of streets in old areas like Westminster and the City follow the line of medieval streets. Many of the street names, such as The Strand and Fleet Street, have not changed since the Middle Ages. In many other British towns, the layout and the names of the streets go back to medieval times.

The birth of modern English

London is a rich mixture of different people, but most of them use the English language when talking to each other. The modern form of English developed during the Middle Ages. The Normans added French and Latin words to the Old English language that was spoken in 1066. The result was the birth of modern English.

Country roots

Many of these medieval features can be seen in towns and cities outside London. The impact of the Middle Ages can also be seen in the countryside. Although nearly all the medieval 'open fields' have gone, many modern hedges still follow the line of medieval boundaries. Most villages are on the site of a medieval village; and many of their names can be found in the Domesday Book of 1086. In most villages the largest building is the church. The architecture of many churches has not changed since medieval times. Often, there is a 'manor house' near the church, on the site of the house built by the local landlord in medieval times.

Attainment target grid

This grid is designed to indicate the varying emphases on attainment targets in the questions in each unit. It is not to be interpreted as a rigid framework, but as a simple device to help the teacher plan the study unit.

X	some focus
XX	strong focus
XXX	main focus

		AT 1 a	AT 1 b	AT 1 c	AT 2	AT 3
1	Britain before the Norman Conquest					
2	1066: the Conquest	X	XXX		X	X
3	The Normans in power				XXX	XX
4	Kings and Parliaments	XXX		X		
5	Murder in the cathedral		XXX		XX	X
6	Bad King John?				XX	XXX
7	England and the Celtic lands	XXX		X		X
8	Bannockburn		XXX			X
9	The Peasants' Revolt of 1381		XX	XXX	X	X
10	Richard III: hero or villain?				XX	XXX
11	The countryside				XXX	XX
12	Work without pay			XX	XXX	X
13	Women in the countryside			X		XXX
14	The changing face of town life	XXX	X		XXX	XX
15	Law and order		X	XXX		X
16	Yorkshire 1219			XXX		X
17	The power of the Church		X	XX	XXX	X
18	Monks and nuns			XX		XXX
19	Looking after the sick			XXX		X
20	The Black Death			XX		XXX
21	Building the castles and cathedrals			XXX		XX
22	The English language	XXX				
23	Two English writers			XXX		X
24	A medieval legacy					

N

Kirkwall

Elgin
Kinloss
Aberdeen
SCOTLAND
Brechin
St. Andrews
Dunblane
Glasgow
Edinburgh
Melrose
Sweetheart
Carlisle
Durham

Main cathedral or monastery

† Cistercian monastery

University

✕ Battle

Armagh
Boyle
IRELAND
Dublin
Cashel

St. Asaph
Bangor
WALES
St. David's
Strata Florida
Hereford
Tintern
Llandaff
Bristol
Wells
Salisbury
Exeter

ENGLAND
Byland
Ripon   † Rievaulx
Fountains
York   ✕ Stamford Bridge (1066)

Lincoln

Lichfield   ✕ Bosworth   Norwich
              (1485)
Worcester   Ely
            Cambridge
Gloucester
            Oxford
London   Canterbury
Winchester   Rochester
                        Dover
Chichester
            Hastings
            (1066)

English Channel

Rouen

NORMANDY

0   100 km

Medieval Britain

Index